# SPANISH IN 60 DAYS

## LA CUCARACHA SARA

Printed in the United States of America.

First Edition 2023

ISBN: 979-8-9894433-0-7 (print)

# Introduction

**Hola! Yo soy La Cucaracha Sara and I teach Mexican slang.**

Learn Spanish quickly while having fun.

**Textbooks and apps often teach you grammar and vocabulary that does not reflect how native speakers communicate...until now.
In this book you will learn Spanish that actually matters!**

> " Spanish lessons but let's make it
> **MEXICAN SLANG** "

**BIENVENIDOS!**

# TABLE OF CONTENTS

# Planeador Semanal
## weekly planner

### Semana de:
week of:

lunes
Monday

martes
tuesday

miercoles
Wednesday

jueves
thursday

viernes
Friday

sabado
Saturday

domingo
Sunday

Notes
**Notas**

## Cosas que hacer
things to do

## Recordatorio
reminder

5

# Here are some examples to use in your weekly planner

**cocinar**
(koh-seen-ar)
cook

**ir al mercado**
(eer ahl mehr-kah-doh)
go to the market

**lavar la ropa**
(lah-var lah roh-pah)
laundry

**limpiar la casa**
(leem-pee-ar lah kah-sah)
clean the house

**regar las plantas**
(reh-gar lahs plahn-tahs)
water the plants

**lavar el carro/coche**
(lah-var ehl cah-rroh/koh-cheh
carwash

**trabajo**
(trah-bah-ho)
work

**junta con**
(hoon-tah kohn)
meeting with

**reunion**
(reh-oo-neon)
reunion

**clase**
(klah-seh)
class

**escuela**
(es-kweh-lah)
school

**estudiar**
(es-to-dee-ar)
study

**leer**
(leh-er)
read

**lecciones**
(lehk-syoh-nehs)
lessons

**ejercisio**
(eh-hehr-see-syoh)
exercise

**ir al gymnacio**
(ir ahl heem-nah-syoh)
go to the gym

**ir al mecanico**
(ir ahl meh-kah-nee-coh)
go to the mechanic

| | |
|---|---|
| **cita con el doctor**<br>(see-tah kohn ehl dohk-tor) | doctor's appointment |
| **cita con el dentista**<br>(see-tah kohn ehl dehn-tees-tah) | dentist appointment |
| **sesion de terapia**<br>(seh-syoh deh teh-rah-pee-ah) | therapy session |
| **meditación**<br>(meh-dee-tah-syon) | meditation |
| **corte de pelo**<br>(kohr-teh deh pehl-loh) | haircut |
| **cita de pestañas**<br>(see-tah deh pehs-tahn-yahs) | lash appointment |
| **cita de uñas**<br>(see-tah deh oo-nyahs) | nail appointment |
| **spa**<br>(spa) | spa |
| **cena con**<br>(seh-nah kohn) | dinner with |
| **cumpleaños**<br>(koom-pleh-ah-nyohs) | birthday |
| **aniversario**<br>(ah-nee-vehr-sari-oh) | anniversary |
| **vacaciones**<br>(vah-kah-see-oh-ness) | vacations |
| **concierto**<br>(kohn-see-ehr-toh) | concert |
| **llamar**<br>(yah-mar) | call |
| **recoger**<br>(reh-koh-hehr) | pick up |
| **tomar mas agua**<br>(toh-mar mahs ah-gwah) | drink more water |
| **dormir 8 horas**<br>(dohr-meer ocho oh-rahs ) | sleep 8 hours |

# ABECEDARIO
## ALPHABET

A (ah ) - sounds like "ah"

B (beh) - sounds like the English "b"

C (seh) - sounds like the English "k". Before "e" or "i", it sounds like an "s"

D (deh) - sounds like the English "d"

E (eh ) - sounds like "eh"

F (efe) - sounds like the English "f"

G (heh) - sounds like the English "h" or "g"

H (ahche) - silent

I (ee) - sounds like "ee"

J (hota) - sounds like the English "h"

K (kah) - sounds like the English "k"

L (eh-leh) - sounds like the English "l"

M (eh-meh) - sounds like the English "m"

N (eh-neh) - sounds like the English "n"

Ñ (eh-nye) - sounds like "ny" (caNYon)

O (oh) - sounds like the "o" in orange

P (peh) - sounds like the English "p"

Q (ku) - sounds like the English "k"

R (eh-reh) - sounds like a harsh English "r"

S (eh-seh) - sounds like the English "s"

T (teh) - sounds like the English "t"

U (oo) - sounds like "oo"

V (veh) - sound like the English "b"

W (doble veh) - sounds like the English "w"

X (eh-kees) - sounds like the English "h" or "s"

Y (yeh / ee gryeh-gah) - sounds like the English "y"

Z (zeta) - sounds like the English "z"

# VOCALES
## VOWELS

A - ah

E - eh

I - ee

O - oh

U - oo

# ABECEDARIO
## ALPHABET

- The letter "g" is pronounced like the "h" in "huge" before "e" or "i" and like the "g" in "go" before "a", "o", or "u".
- The letter "h" is silent in Spanish.
- The letter "j" is pronounced like the "h".
- The letters "ll" are pronounced like the "y" in "yellow".
- The letter "ñ" is pronounced like the "ny" in "canyon".
- The letters "rr" are trilled with the tip of the tongue.

**gente - (hen-teh)**
people
**girasol - (hee-rah-sol)**
sunflower
**gasolina - (gah-so-lina)**
gasoline
**gozar - (go-zar)**
enjoy
**gusta - (goos-ta)**
like

**jugo - (hoo-go)**
juice
**jabón - (ha-bhon)**
soap
**jefe - (hefe)**
male boss
**jirafa - (hee-ra-fah)**
giraffe

**lluvia - (yuvi-ah)**
rain
**llave - (yah-beh)**
key
**llamar - (yah-mahr)**
to call
**calle - (ka-ye)**
street

**niño - (nee-nyo)**
boy
**niña - (nee-nya)**
girl
**español - (es-pah-nyol)**
spanish
**años - (anyos)**
years
**mañana - (mah-nyana)**
tomorrow
**piña - (pee-nya)**
pineapple

## DIAS DE LA SEMANA
### DAYS OF THE WEEK

**lunes - Monday**
(loo-nehs)

**martes - Tuesday**
(mar-tehs)

**miércoles - Wednesday**
(mee-ehr-kohl-ehs)

**jueves - Thursday**
(hoo-e-vehs)

**viernes - Friday**
(vee-ehr-nehs)

**sábado - Saturday**
(sah-bah-doh)

**domingo - Sunday**
(doe-meen-goh)

### MESES
### MONTHS

- **enero - January**
  (eh-neh-roh)
- **febrero - February**
  (feh-brair-oh)
- **marzo - March**
  (mar-soh)
- **abril - April**
  (ah-bril)
- **mayo - May**
  (mah-yoh)
- **junio - June**
  (hoo-nee-oh)
- **julio - July**
  (hoo-lee-oh)
- **agosto - August**
  (ah-gohs-toh)
- **septiembre - September**
  (sehpt-ee-ehm-breh)
- **octubre - October**
  (ock-too-breh)
- **noviembre - November**
  (noe-vee-em-breh)
- **diciembre - December**
  (dee-see-em-breh)

**El lunes tengo una cita con el doctor a las 3 de la tarde.**
Monday I have a doctor's appointment at 3 in the afternoon.

**El martes tengo una reunión con el equipo de ventas a las 10 de la mañana.**
On Tuesday I have a meeting with the sales team at 10 in the morning.

**Trabajo los fines de semana pero descanso los miércoles y jueves.**
I work weekends but I have Wednesdays and Thursdays off.

**rojo - red**
(roh-hoh)

**naranja - orange**
(nah-rahn-hah)

**amarillo - yellow**
(ah-mah-ree-yoh)

**verde - green**
(vehr-deh)

**azul - blue**
(ah-sool)

**morado - purple**
(moh-rah-doh)

**rosa - pink**
(roh-sah)

**marrón - brown**
(mah-rohn)

**café - brown**
(ka-feh)

**gris - gray**
(grees)

**negro - black**
(neh-gro)

**blanco - white**
(blahn-koh)

**beige - beige**
(beysh)

**dorado - golden**
(doh-rah-doh)

**plateado - silver**
(plah-teh-ah-doh)

## COLORES
### COLORS

# LAS PARTES DEL CUERPO
## BODY PARTS

**la cabeza - head**
(lah kah-beh-sah)
**el cuello - neck**
(ehl kweh-yoh)
**los hombros - shoulders**
(los ohm-bros)
**los brazos -arms**
(los brah-sos)
**las manos - hands**
(las mah-nohs)
**el pecho - chest**
(ehl peh-choh)
**el abdomen - abdomen**
(ehl ahb-doh-men)
**las caderas - hips**
(las kah-deh-ras)
**las piernas - legs**
(las pyeh-rnas)
**los pies - feet**
(los pee-eh-s)

**la cara - face**
(lah ka-rah)
**los ojos - eyes**
(los oh-hos)
**la nariz - nose**
(lah nah-rees)
**la boca - mouth**
(lah boh-kah)
**la lengua - tongue**
(la lehn-gwah)
**los dientes - teeth**
(los dyehn-tes)
**el cerebro - brain**
(el seh-reh-broh)
**el corazón - heart**
(el koh-rah-sohn)
**los pulmones - lungs**
(los pool-moh-nes)
**los riñones - kidneys**
(los ree-nyoh-nes)

**la espalda - back**
(la eh-spal-dah)
**el estómago - stomach**
(ehl es-toh-mah-goh)
**los músculos - muscles**
(los moos-koo-lohs)
**las uñas - nails**
(las oon-yas)
**el cabello - hair**
(ehl kah-beh-yoh)
**la piel - skin**
(lah pyel)
**el oído - ear**
(ehl o-ee-doh)
**la rodilla - knee**
(lah roh-dee-yah)
**el codo - elbow**
(ehl koh-doh)

**el dedo - finger**
(ehl deh-doh)
**el dedo del pie - toe**
(el deh-doh del pee-eh)
**el hueso - bone**
(ehl weh-soh)
**la vejiga - bladder**
(lah veh-hee-gah)
**el hígado - liver**
(ehl ee-gah-doh)
**el intestino - intestine**
(ehl in-tes-tee-no)
**el páncreas - pancreas**
(ehl pahn-kreh-ahs)
**la vena - vein**
(lah veh-nah)

11

# NÚMEROS
## NUMBERS

0 - cero (seh-roh)
1 - uno (oo-no)
2 - dos (dohs)
3 - tres (trehs)
4 - cuatro (kwah-troh)
5 - cinco (seen-koh)
6 - seis (seh-ehs)
7 - siete (see-eh-teh)
8 - ocho (oh-choh)
9 - nueve (nweh-veh)
10 - diez (dyehs)
11 - once (ohnce)
12 - doce (doh-seh)
13 - trece (treh-seh)
14 - catorce (kah-tor-seh)
15 - quince (keen-seh)

16 - dieciséis (dyeh-see-seh-ehs)
17 - diecisiete (dyeh-see-see-eh-teh)
18 - dieciocho (dyeh-see-oh-choh)
19 - diecinueve (dyeh-see-nweh-veh)
20 - veinte (vayn-teh)
21 - veintiuno (vayn-tee-oo-no)
22 - veintidós (vayn-tee-dohs)
23 - veintitrés (vayn-tee-trehs)
24 - veinticuatro (vayn-tee-kwah-troh)
25 - veinticinco (vayn-tee-seen-koh)
26 - veintiséis (vayn-tee-seh-ehs)
27 - veintisiete (vayn-tee-see-eh-teh)
28 - veintiocho (vayn-tee-oh-choh)
29 - veintinueve (vayn-tee-nweh-veh)
30 - treinta (trehn-tah)
31 - treinta y uno (trehn-tah ee oo-no)
32 - treinta y dos (trehn-tah ee dohs)
33 - treinta y tres (trehn-tah ee trehs)
34 - treinta y cuatro (trehn-tah ee kwah-troh)
35 - treinta y cinco (trehn-tah ee seen-koh)
36 - treinta y seis (trehn-tah ee seh-ehs)
37 - treinta y siete (trehn-tah ee see-eh-teh)
38 - treinta y ocho (trehn-tah ee oh-choh)
39 - treinta y nueve (trehn-tah ee nweh-veh)
40 - cuarenta (kwah-rehn-tah)
41 - cuarenta y uno (kwah-rehn-tah ee oo-no)
42 - cuarenta y dos (kwah-rehn-tah ee dohs)
43 - cuarenta y tres (kwah-rehn-tah ee trehs)
44 - cuarenta y cuatro (kwah-rehn-tah ee kwah-troh)
45 - cuarenta y cinco (kwah-rehn-tah ee seen-koh)
46 - cuarenta y seis (kwah-rehn-tah ee seh-ehs)
47 - cuarenta y siete (kwah-rehn-tah ee see-eh-teh)
48 - cuarenta y ocho (kwah-rehn-tah ee oh-choh)
49 - cuarenta y nueve (kwah-rehn-tah ee nweh-veh)
50 - cincuenta (seen-kwehn-tah)

100 - cien (see-ehn), ciento (see-en-toh)
200 - doscientos (dohs-see-ehn-tohs)
300 - trescientos (trehs-see-ehn-tohs)
400 - cuatrocientos (kwah-troh-see-ehn-tohs)
500 - quinientos (kee-nee-ehn-tohs)
600 - seiscientos (sey-see-ehn-tohs)
700 - setecientos (seh-teh-see-ehn-tohs)
800 - ochocientos (oh-choh-see-ehn-tohs)
900 - novecientos (noh-veh-see-ehn-tohs)

1000 - mil (meel)
2,000 - dos mil (dohs meel)
3,000 - tres mil (trehs meel)
4,000 - cuatro mil (kwah-troh meel)
5,000 - cinco mil (seen-koh meel)
6,000 - seis mil (seh-ehs meel)
7,000 - siete mil (see-eh-teh meel)
8,000 - ocho mil (oh-choh meel)
9,000 - nueve mil (nweh-veh meel)
10,000 - diez mil (dyehs meel)

100,000 - cien mil (see-ehn meel)
200,000 - doscientos mil (dohs-see-ehn-tohs meel)
300,000 - trescientos mil (trehs-see-ehn-tohs meel)
400,000 - cuatrocientos mil (kwah-troh-see-ehn-tohs meel)
500,000 - quinientos mil (kee-nee-ehn-tohs meel)
600,000 - seiscientos mil (sey-see-ehn-tohs meel)
700,000 - setecientos mil (seh-teh-see-ehn-tohs meel)
800,000 - ochocientos mil (oh-choh-see-ehn-tohs meel)
900,000 - novecientos mil (noh-veh-see-ehn-tohs meel)
1,000,000 - un millón (oon mee-yohn )

To form numbers larger than 100, you can use a combination of the words for the
**hundreds, tens, ones (units).**

135 is **ciento treinta y cinco** in Spanish
(one hundred thirty-five)

847 is **ochocientos cuarenta y siete** in Spanish
(eight hundred forty-seven)

To form numbers larger than 1000, you can use a combination of the words for the

**thousands, hundreds, tens, ones (units)**

10,235 is **diez mil doscientos treinta y cinco** in Spanish
(literally ten thousand two hundred thirty-five).

3,481 is **tres mil cuatrocientos ochenta y uno** in Spanish
(literally three thousand four hundred eighty-one).

## Test your understanding

*Write the correct translation*

1. la mano -
2. la cara -
3. las piernas -
4. la boca-
5. los musculos-
6. la cabeza-

7. azul -
8. morado -
9. rojo-
10. verde-
11. amarillo-
12. rosa-

*Match each number*

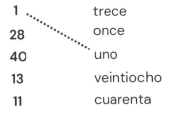

| | |
|---|---|
| 1 | trece |
| 28 | once |
| 40 | uno |
| 13 | veintiocho |
| 11 | cuarenta |

*Match each day of the week*

| | |
|---|---|
| lunes | Wednesday |
| martes | Sunday |
| miercoles | Friday |
| jueves | Tuesday |
| viernes | Saturday |
| sabado | Monday |
| domingo | Thursday |

*Write the correct number*

1. 3 is _____ in Spanish
   (three)

2. 12 is _____ in Spanish
   (twelve)

3. 342 is _____ in Spanish
   (three hundred forty-two)

4. 906 is _____ in Spanish
   (nine hundred six )

5. 1,029 is _____ in Spanish
   (one thousand twenty-nine)

6. 4,471 is _____ in Spanish
   (four thousand four hundred seventy-one)

7. quinientos ochenta y cuatro mil doscientos = <u>584,200</u>

8. doscientos sesenta y siete mil novecientos ochenta y cuatro = _____

9. ciento cuarenta y cinco = _____

10. seis mil = _____

14

# MY NOTES

# Planeador Semanal
### weekly planner

## Semana de:
### Week of:

**lunes**
Monday

**martes**
tuesday

**miercoles**
Wednesday

**jueves**
thursday

**viernes**
Friday

**sabado**
Saturday

**domingo**
Sunday

## Cosas que hacer
things to do

## Recordatorio
reminder

Notes
## Notas

# MEXICAN SLANG

*Madres* literally translates to 'mothers' but once you put it in different phrases it changes the meaning.

"me vale madres" literally translates to 'it is worth a mother', what we mean is
(meh vah-leh mah-thres)
'I don't care, idgf'.

"chinga tu madre" literally translates to 'fuck your mother', this phrase is used
(cheen-gah too mah-thre)
just like "fuck you" is used in English.

"desmadre" literally translates to 'unmothered', used to describe something
(dess-mah-thre)
hectic or chaotic.

"a toda madre" literally translates to 'a full mother', used to describe a badass
(ah toh-dah ma-thre)
time.

"te voy a romper la madre" literally translates to 'I'm going to break your
(teh voy ah romp-er lah mah-thre)
mother', what we mean is 'I'm going to fuck you up'

*Padre* literally means father, but "que padre" can mean how cool, how awesome.
Chido / chida also means cool.

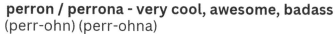

perron / perrona - very cool, awesome, badass
(perr-ohn) (perr-ohna)
> You can use perron / perrona to describe a situation, a thing, or a person.
> If the noun is masculine = perron. If the noun is feminine = perrona.

# MEXICAN SLANG

**la mera mera / el mero mero- the big boss, the main character**
(lah merah merah) (ehl meroh-meroh)

**jefe / jefa- literally "boss" often used as dad(jefe) or mom(jefa)**
(hef-eh) (hef-ah)

**tocayo / tocaya- someone with the same name as you. Namesake**
(toka-yo) (toka-yah)

> It is very common to address someone with the same name as you as "mi (my) tocayo / tocaya"

**carnal- brother or bro**
(car-nhal)

**carnala- sister or sis**
(car-nala)

**compa- male friend, buddy**
(com- pah)

**cuate- literally "twin" used as male friend or buddy**
(ku- ah- teh)

**morro- a young male, dude**
(moh-rro)

**morra- a young female, a girl**
(moh-rra)

**jaina- a female, girlfriend or wife**
(hi-nah)

**chavo- a young male, dude**
(cha-voh)

**chava- a young female**
(cha-vah)

**escuincle/ escuincla- a spoiled brat, a kid**
(esk-winkleh) / (esk-winklah)

**mocoso /mocosa- a spoiled brat, someone who behaves badly, "snotty kid"**
(moco-so) / (moco-sah)

# MEXICAN SLANG

**fresa- "strawberry" used to describe someone who is snobby or spoiled, bougie**
(freh-sah)

**me choca- translates to 'it bumped me', meaning, it irks me, I don't like it, I hate it.**
(meh choka)

**me caga- translates to 'it shits on me' but what we mean is, I hate it.**
(meh ka-gha)

**"me caga" and "me choca" mean the same thing but "me caga" is vulgar.
"Me choca" is not vulgar.**

**no la cagües - don't shit on it, don't fuck it up**
(no lah ka-gues)

**la cagüe - I shat on it, I fucked up**
(lah ka-gue)

**qué onda- what's up**
(ke on-dah)

**qué tranza- what's up**
(ke trahn-za)

**qué pedo- literally "what fart" used as what's up or what's the problem**
(ke pedo)

**ah huevo- hell yeah, no doubt. Huevo literally translates to 'egg'**
(ah weh-bho)

**aguas- literally "waters", slang for watch out or be careful**
(ah-gwas)

**un paro- a favor**
(un pah-ro)

**chido / chida- cool**
(chee-doh) (chee-dah)

Learn more about masculine and feminine nouns in week 4.

If the noun is masculine you can described it as "chido".

If the noun is feminine you can described it as "chida".

# MEXICAN SLANG

**qué padre- how cool, how awesome**
(ke pa-thre)

**muy padre- very cool, very awesome. Literally translates to "very father"**
(muy pa-thre)

**de pelos- literally "of hairs" used to describe something fun or amazing**
(deh peh-los)

> La boda estuvo de pelos - The wedding was amazing.

**sale- deal, ok, bet**
(sah-leh)

**me late- I like it, I'm feeling it**
(meh lah-teh)

**buena onda- good vibes, good energy**
(buena on-dah)

**cabron / cabrona - a badass person, fucker, bastard**
(ka-bronh) (ka-brona)

> **A situation can be 'cabron' - fucking tough**
> - Como va la chamba? - How's work?
> - Pues esta cabron - Well, it's fucking-tough
>
> **It can also be an expression. Ah cabron! - Oh shit!**
> *sees something shocking*
> **"AH CABRON!"**

**no te agüites - don't get upset, don't let it get to you, cheer up**
(no teh ah-gwee-tehs)

**no te rajes - don't give up, don't back down**
(no teh rah-hehs)

**no me rajo - I don't give up**
(no meh rra-ho)

**no se rajen - all of you don't give up**
(no seh rra-hen)

**no se rajaron - they didn't give up**
(no seh rraha-ron)

**estas bien bueno / buena: you are so hot, you are so fine**
(estas bee-en boo-eh-no)  (boo-eh-na)

# MEXICAN SLANG

**mi media naranja- "my half orange"  but it's used as my soulmate or my other half**
(mee meh-dia naran-ha)

**mi vida- literally "my life"  used as my love, my everything**
(mee vee-dah)

> "Mi vida" can be used in a romantic way or friendly way
> (towards children or friends).

**apapachar- to snuggle or to cuddle**
(ah-pah-pah-char)

> From the Nahuatl word *apapacho* which means "caress with the soul".

**nene- babyboy**
(nhe-nhe)

> Can be used towards an actual baby boy or in a romantic way.

**nena- babygirl**
(nhe-na)

> Can be used towards an actual baby girl or in a romantic way.

**mijo- derived from "mi hijo" which means "my son" used as honey, dear, sweetie**
(meeho)

> Mijo can be used in a friendly way or in a romantic way.

**mija- "mi hija" which means "my daughter" used as honey, dear, sweetie**
(meeha)

> Mija can be used in a friendly way or in a romantic way.

**papi- synonym for babe**
(papi)

> Papi can also be a synonym for "mijo". It's very common for parents to call their child "papi" as in honey, dear, sweetie.
> Papi literally translates to "daddy".
> Can be used towards your actual dad, in a romantic way, or a friendly way.

**mami- synonym for babe**
(mami)

> Mami can also be a synonym for "mija". It's very common for parents to call their child "mami" as in honey, dear, sweetie.
> Mami literally translates to "mommy".
> Can be used towards your actual mom, in a romantic way, or a friendly way

# MEXICAN SLANG

**papacito- hot daddy, an attractive male**
(papa-cito)

**mamacita- lil mama, an attractive female**
(mama-cita)

**viejo / vieja- old, often used as a term of endearment towards your partner**
(vieho) (vieha)

>"Mi viejo" means "my old man".
>"Mi vieja" means "my old lady".

**ruco- old man, a male. Can be used towards your romantic**
(ruko)                    **partner as "mi ruco"** (my man)

**ruca- old woman, a female. Can be used towards your romantic**
(ruka)                    **partner as "mi ruca"** (my women)

**tipazo / tipaza: great guy, great girl**
(tee-pah-so) (tee-pah-sah)

**ligar - literally "to bind" used  as a synonym for flirting, hooking up**
(lee-ghar)

**chisme- gossip, rumor, "the tea"**
(cheese-meh)

**chismoso / chismosa-  a loud mouth, someone who likes to spread gossip**
(cheese-moso) (cheese-mosa)

**metiche- a nosy person**
(meh-tee-che)

**berrinche- tantrum, an outburst**
(berin-che)

**bájale a tu pedo- "tone down your fart" used as "don't come at me like  that",**
(baha-leh ah too pedo)          **"tone it down"**

**armar un pancho- making a scene, being dramatic, creating an argument**
(ar-mar un pancho)

**caer gordo / gorda- literally "to fall fat", describes a dislike to someone or something**
(kah-er gordo)  (gorda)

# MEXICAN SLANG

**fodongo / fodonga- bummy, musty, someone who does not take care of their hygiene**
(fo-don-goh) (fo-don-gah)

**carcacha- piece of junk, scrap**
(car-ka-cha)

**chafa- cheap, low quality**
(cha-fa)

**ojete- an asshole, someone who is disliked**
(oh-heh-teh)

**maldito / maldita- a vile person**
(mal-dito)  (mal-dita)

**imbécil- a fool, idiot**
(eem-becil)

**rabo verde- literally "green tail" used to describe a pervert or creep**
(rah-boh ver-deh)

**perra- bitch**
(peh-rrah)

**puta- whore**
(poo-tah)

**pinche - fucking (adjective) or someone who is stingy**
(pinch-eh)

> Está bien <u>pinche</u> caliente afuera. - It's so <u>fucking</u> hot out.
>
> No seas <u>pinche</u>, comparte con los demas. - Don't be <u>stingy</u>, share with others.

**pendejo- male dumbass / idiot**
(pen-deh-ho)

**pendeja- female dumbass / idiot**
(pen-deh-ha)

**pendejadas - dumbass things**
(pen-deh-hadas)

**wey / güey- dummy. It can be used as "bro" or "dude"**
(wey)

# MEXICAN SLANG

**no mames- literally " don't suck" but it means "no way!", "for real?", "what the hell!"**
(no mah-mess)

**no manches- literally "don't stain" it means the same as "no mames" but it's less vulg.**
(no man-ches)

**chale - hell no, damn, showing disappointment, anger, or annoyance**
(cha-leh)

**cómo chingas: you are fucking annoying**
(coh-moh chin-ghas)

**cómo chingan: you all are fucking annoying**
(coh-moh chin-ghan)

**qué chingaos / qué chingados- what the fuck (WTF)**
(khe chin-gha-os) (khe chin-gah-dos)

> Qué chingaos es eso? - Wtf is that?
> Qué chingaos fue eso? - Wtf was that?
> Qué chingaos quieres? - Wtf do you want?

**chingadera / chingaderas- the fucking thing(s)**
(chin-gha-dhera) (chin-gha-dheras)

> Esta chingadera no sirve. - This fucking thing doesn't work.
> Pásame la chingadera. - Pass me the fucking thing.

**en chinga: fucking fast, moving really quick**
(en chin-gah)

**una chinga- a fucking beating**
(una chin-gah)

**a la chingada: to hell, fuck it / fuck off**
(ah lah chin-gahda)

> Vete a la chingada. - Go to hell, fuck off.

**estoy hasta la madre / estoy hasta la chingada**
> I'm fucking tired
> I'm fucking fed up
> I'm fucking overwelmed

# MEXICAN SLANG

**un rollo - something annoying, complicated or frustrating "it's a mess", "it's a pain in the neck"**
(un roh-yo)

Fue un rollo encontrar tu departamento. — It was a pain in the neck finding your apartment.

**pesado- literally "heavy" used to describe annoying, rude, or offensive people, or experiences**
(peh-sa-doh)

Tuve un dia <u>pesado.</u> — I've had an <u>annoying</u> day.

Los chistes de Laura son un poco <u>pesados</u>. — Laura's jokes are a bit <u>offensive</u>.

**dando lata - to be annoying**
(dandoh lata)

**latoso / latosa - annoying**
(lah-toso) (lah-tosa)

No seas <u>latoso/latosa.</u> - Don't be <u>annoying</u>.

**caga palos- shit sticks. Someone that is difficult or unpleasant**
(ka-gah palos)

**gacho / gacha- something or someone that is unpleasant or uncool**
(gah-cho) (gah-cha)

**baboso / babosa- a moron. Literal translation is "slimy" or "slobbery"**
(bah-boso) (bah-bosa)

**mamón/ mamona- sucker, someone who is overly attentive to their own needs, a jerk**
(mah-mon) (mah-mona)

**culero / culera- an asshole, someone who is rude or disrespectful**
(coo-lero) (coo-lera)

**codo/ coda- someone who is stingy with money. Codo in Spanish is elbow**
(koh-doh) (koh-dah)

25

# MEXICAN SLANG

**estoy pedo / peda- I'm drunk. Pedo literally translates to "fart"**
(ehs-toy pedo) (peda)

**chela- beer, chelas means "beers"**
(che-lah)

**pistear - to drink an alcoholic beverage**
(pis-teh-ar)

> estoy pisteando - I'm drinking
>
> estas pisteando - you're drinking
>
> estamos pisteando - we're drinking
>
> estan pisteando - they're drinking
>
> vamos a pistear - let's go drink

**crudo / cruda- hangover. Literally translates to "raw"**
(croo-doh) (croo-dah)

> Amanecí <u>crudo</u> / <u>cruda</u>. - I woke up <u>hungover</u>.

**huateque / guateque - a party, a celebration**
(gwah-teh- ke)

**malacopa- someone who does not know how to drink and/or gets drunk easily. A lightweight**
(mala-copa)

**caile- pull up, come through**
(kai-leh)

**algo leve- something light or easy**
(al-go leh-veh)

**jaladas- synonym to the phrase "pulling my leg", fake news, lies, exaggerating**
(haladas)

**dejar plantado- to stand someone up, to leave someone waiting**
(deh-har plan-tado)

**carrilla- teasing**
(kah-reeya)

**feria- money**
(feh-ria)

# MEXICAN SLANG

**chota- police**
(cho-tah)

**un chorro- a shit-ton**
(un cho-rro)

| | | |
|---|---|---|
| Tengo un <u>chorro</u> de trabajo. | - | I have a <u>shit-ton</u> of work |
| Había un <u>chorro</u> de gente en la playa. | - | There was a <u>shit-ton</u> of people at the beach. |

**ya valió- it is over, it is busted or the opportunity is gone**
(ya va-leo)

**ni madres: no way, hell no**
(nee ma-thres)

**me vale- I don't care, I don't give a damn**
(meh vah-leh)

**me vale verga- literally "it's worth a dick" used as "I don't give a fuck"**
(meh vah-leh ver-gah)

| | | |
|---|---|---|
| Me <u>vale verga</u> lo que digan de mi. | - | <u>I don't give a fuck</u> what they say about me. |

**vete a la verga- literally "go to the dick" used as "go to hell" "fuck off"**
(veh-teh ah la ver-gah)

**ponte vergas- toughen up, be wise**
(pon-teh ver-gahs)

# MY FAVORITE SLANG PHRASES

# Planeador Semanal
### weekly planner

## Semana de:
### Week of:

| lunes |
| Monday |

| martes |
| Tuesday |

| miercoles |
| Wednesday |

| jueves |
| Thursday |

| viernes |
| Friday |

| sabado |
| Saturday |

| domingo |
| Sunday |

## Cosas que hacer
### things to do

## Recordatorio
### reminder

Notes
**Notas**

29

# FOLLOW ME

Instagram @la.cucaracha.sara

TikTok @la.cucaracha.sara

YouTube @la.cucaracha.sara

Pinterest @lacucarachasara

Web www.glotmour.com

**Me llamo** _____ **¡Mucho gusto!**
My name is _____ Nice to meet you!

Don't just say *hola* all the time. Try these greetings.

**¿Qué onda?**
(ke on-dah)
**What's up?**

**¿Qué me cuentas?**
(ke meh koo-en-tas)
**How's it going?**

**¿Cómo estás?**
(komo es-tas)
**How are you?**

**¿Qué tal?**
(ke tal)
**What's up?**

**¿Quiubo?**
(kee-yu-boh)
**What's up?**

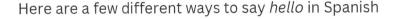

Here are a few different ways to say *hello* in Spanish

 (oh-lah)

This is the most common way to greet someone in Spanish, which means hello or hi.

**Buenos días** (bweh-nohs dee-ahs)
Good morning. It is typically used during the daytime.

**Buenas tardes** (bweh-nahs tar-dehs)
Good afternoon. It is typically used in the early afternoon.

**Buenas noches** (bweh-nahs noh-chehs)
Good evening. It is typically used in the evening.

**Hola de nuevo** (oh-lah deh nweh-voh)
Hello again.

**Buen día** (bwehn dee-ah)
Good day.

**Saludos** (sah-loo-dohs)
Greetings.

**Hola a todos** (oh-lah ah toh-dohs)
Hello everyone.

**Buenos días, señor** (bweh-nohs dee-ahs, seh-nyor)
Good morning, sir. This is a formal way to greet someone in the morning.

**Buenos días, señora** (bweh-nohs dee-ahs, seh-nyor-ah)
Good morning ma'am. This is a formal way to greet someone in the morning.

**Buenas tardes, señor** (bweh-nahs tar-dehs, seh-nyor)
Good afternoon, sir. This is a formal way to greet someone in the afternoon.

**Buenas tardes, señora** (bweh-nahs tar-dehs, seh-nyor-ah)
Good afternoon, ma'am. This is a formal way to greet someone in the afternoon.

**Buenas noches, señor/señora** (bweh-nahs noh-chehs, seh-nyor / seh-nyor-ah)
This means "good evening, sir/ma'am" and is a formal way to greet someone in the evening.

**Ser** & **Estar** are irregular verbs, both mean **to be**.
**Soy** & **Estoy** mean **I am**.

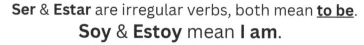

# Ser
## vs
# Estar

Use "soy" when talking about your
- characteristics
- occupation
- orgin

Use "estoy" when talking about your
- actions
- emotions
- location

Things that make someones who they are & are unlikely to change. Think "permanent"

¿Donde estas?
Where are you?

¿Que haces?
What are you doing?

¿Cómo estás?
How are you?

will always be answered with "estoy"

Often the pronoun **yo** (I) is omitted because **estoy / soy** will always mean *I am* weather **yo** is included or not.

Write *soy* as you read each sentence out loud.

¿Quien eres?          answer with          **Soy**

**Who are you?**                              **soy** means **I am**

_s o y_    _____
            your name

_s o y_    **fiel**                          I am loyal
            (fee-ehl)

---------   **honesto**                       I am honest *male*
            (ohn-eh-stoh)

---------   **honesta**                       I am honest *female*
            (ohn-eh-stah)

---------   **valiente**                      I am brave
            (vah-lee-ehn-teh)

---------   **inteligente**                   I am smart
            (een-teh-lee-hehn-teh)

---------   **amable**                        I am nice
            (ah-mah-bleh)

---------   **humilde**                       I am humbe
            (oo-meel-deh)

---------   **mujer**                         I am a women
            (moo-hair)

---------   **hombre**                        I am a man
            (ohm-breh)

---------   **madre**                         I am a mother
            (mah-thre)

---------   **padre**                         I am a father
            (pah- thre)

---------   **guapo**                         I am handsome *male*
            (gwah-poh)

---------   **guapa**                         I am pretty *female*
            (gwah-pah)

---------   **jugador de futbol**             I am a soccer player
            (hoo-gah-dohr deh foot-bohl)

---------   **mariachi**                      I am a mariachi artist
            (mah-ree-achi)

34

Write *soy* as you read each sentence out loud.

## ¿De dónde eres?
## Where are you from?

answer with  **Soy**
(soy)

| | | |
|---|---|---|
| _s o y_ | **mexicana**<br>(meh-hee-kah-nah) | I am Mexican female |
| | **mexicano**<br>(meh-hee-kah-no) | I am Mexican male |
| | **americano**<br>(ah-meh-ree-kah-no) | I am American male |
| | **americana**<br>(ah-meh-ree-kah-nah) | I am American female |
| | **africano**<br>(ah-free-kah-no) | I am African male |
| | **africana**<br>(ah-free-kah-nah) | I am African female |
| | **africano americano**<br>(ah-free-kah-noh ah-meh-ree-kah-noh) | I am African American |
| | **japones**<br>(hah-poh-nes) | I am Japanese |
| | **dominicano**<br>(doh-mee-nee-kah-noh) | I am Dominican male |
| | **dominicana**<br>(doh-mee-nee-kah-nah) | I am Dominican female |
| | **de Uruguay**<br>(deh uruguay) | I am from Uruguay |
| | **de Mexico**<br>(deh meh-hee-koh) | I am from Mexico |
| | **de Canada**<br>(deh kah-nah-dah) | I am from Canada |
| | **de los Estados Unidos**<br>(deh lohs ehs-tah-dohs oo-nee-dohs) | I am from the USA |
| | **del Reyno Unido**<br>(dehl rey-no oo-nee-doh) | I am from the UK |

¿A qué te dedicas?

**What do you do for a living?**

answer with

**Soy**

I am

| | | |
|---|---|---|
| soy ............ | **enfermero** (ehn-fehr-meh-roh) | I am a nurse   male |
| ............ | **enfermera** (ehn-fehr-meh-rah) | I am a nurse   female |
| ............ | **pediatra** (peh-dee-aht-rah) | I am a pediatrician |
| ............ | **dentista** (dehn-tees-tah) | I am a dentist |
| ............ | **asistente dental** (ah-see-stehn-teh den-tal) | I am a dental assistant |
| ............ | **gerente financiero** (heh-ren-teh  fee-nan-cee-ero) | I am a financial manager |
| ............ | **policia** (poh-lee-see-ah) | I am police officer |
| ............ | **psiquiatra** (see-kee-ah-trah) | I am a psychiatrist |
| ............ | **terapeuta** (teh-rah-peh-oo-tah) | I am a therapist |
| ............ | **ingeniero quimico** (een-heh-nyeh-roh kee-mee-koh) | I am a chemical engineer |
| ............ | **analista** (ah-nah-lees-tah) | I am an analyst |
| ............ | **mecanico** (meh-kah-nee-koh) | I am a mechanic |
| ............ | **modelo** (moh-deh-loh) | I am a model |
| ............ | **estudiante** (eh-stoo-dee-ahn-teh) | I am a student |
| ............ | **mesero** (meh-seh-roh) | I am a waiter |
| ............ | **mesera** (meh-seh-rah) | I am a waitress |

# Here are more examples of career titles

**doctor / doctora**                        **doctor**
(dohk-tor) (dohk-tora)

**medico / medica**                       **physician**
(meh-dee-koh) (meh-dee-kah)

**cirujano / cirujana**                    **surgeon**
(seer-oo-hano)   (seer-oo-ha-na)

**veterinario / veterinaria**           **veterinarian**
(veh-tehr-ee-nahr-ee-oh)(veh-tehr-ee-nahr-ee-ah)

**ingeniero / ingeniera**                 **engineer**
(een-heh-nyeh-roh)(een-heh-nyeh-rah)

**director / directora**                  **director**
(dee-rek-tor) (dee-rek-tora)

**profesor / profesora**                 **professor**
(proh-feh-sor)  (proh-feh-sora)

**maestro / maestra**                   **teacher**
(mah-ehs-troh)  (mah-ehs-trah)

**abogado / abogada**                   **lawyer**
(ah-boh-gah-doh) (ah-boh-gah-dah)

**contador / contadora**                **accountant**
(kohn-tah-dor) (kohn-tah-dora)

**analista financiero /  financiera**    **financial analyst**
(ah-nah-leest-ah fee-nahn-see-ehr-oh)(fee-nahn-see-ehr-ah)

**vendedor / vendedora**                **salesperson**
(vehn-deh-dor) (vehn-deh-dora)

**cocinero / cocinera**                   **cook**
(koh-seen-ehr-oh) (koh-seen-ehr-ah)

**cajero / cajera**                        **cashier**
(kah-heh-roh) (kah-heh-rah)

**conductor / conductora**               **driver**
(kohn-dook-tor) (kohn-dook-tora)

**peluquero / peluquera**                **hairdresser**
(peh-loo-keh-roh)

# **Estoy** also means **I am.**

¿Cómo estás?
**How are you?**    answer with ⇨    **Estoy**
(eh-stoy )

Write *estoy* as you read each sentence out loud.

| estoy | **muy bien** (moo-ee byen) | **I am very well** |
|---|---|---|
| | **alegre** (ah-leh-greh) | **I am cheerful/happy** |
| | **feliz** (feh-lees) | **I am happy** |
| | **motivado** (moh-tee-vah-doh) | **I am motivated** male |
| | **motivada** (moh-tee-vah-dah) | **I am motivated** female |
| | **ocupado** (oh-koo-pah-doh) | **I am busy** male |
| | **ocupada** (oh-koo-pah-dah) | **I am busy** female |
| | **aburrido** (ah-boo-rree-doh) | **I am bored** male |
| | **aburrida** (ah-boo-rree-dah) | **I am bored** female |
| | **asustado** (ah-soos-tah-doh) | **I am scared** male |
| | **asustada** (ah-soos-tah-dah) | **I am scared** female |
| | **un poco triste** (oon poh-koh trees-teh) | **I am a bit sad** |
| | **un poquito cansado** (oon poh-kee-toh can-sah-doh) | **I am a little bit tired** male |
| | **un poquito cansada** (oon poh-kee-toh can-sah-dah) | **I am a little bit tired** female |
| | **a todo dar** (ah toh-doh dar) | **I am fantastic** |

# Here are more examples of emotions and feelings

**contento / contenta**                    happy
(kohn-tehn-toh) (kohn-tehn-tah)
**emocionado / emocionada**                excited
(ehm-oh-see-oh-nah-doh) ( ehm-oh-see-oh-nah-dah)
**orgulloso / orgullosa**                  proud
(ohr-goo-yoh-soh) (ohr-goo-yoh-sah)
**agradecido / agradecida**                thankful
(ah-gra-deh-see-doh) (ah-gra-deh-see-dah)
**enamorado / enamorada**                  in love
(ehn-ah-moh-rah-doh)(ehn-ah-moh-rah-dah)
**satisfecho / satisfecha**                satisfied
(sah-tees-feh-cho) (sah-tees-feh-cha)
**sorprendido / sorprendida**              surprised
(sohr-prehn-dee-doh) (sohr-prehn-dee-dah)
**más o menos**                            so so
(mas oh meh-nohs)
**aburrido / aburrida**                    bored
(ah-boo-rree-doh) (ah-boo-rree-dah)
**tranquilo / tranquila**                  calm
(trahn-kee-loh) (trahn-kee-lah)
**relajado / relajada**                    relaxed
(reh-lah-hah-doh) (reh-lah-hah-dah)
**nervioso / nerviosa**                    nervous
(nehr-be-oh-soh) (nehr-be-oh-sah)
**fatal**                                  horrible
(fah-tahl)
**celoso / celosa**                        jealous
(seh-loh-soh) (seh-loh-sah)
**preocupado / preocupada**                worried
(preh-oh-koo-pah-doh) (preh-oh-koo-pah-dah)
**triste**                                 sad
(tree-steh)
**enfadado / enfadada**                    annoyed
(ehn-fah-dah-doh) (ehn-fah-dah-dah)
**frustrado / frustrada**                  frustrated
(froo-strah-doh) (froo-strah-dah)
**ansioso / ansiosa**                      anxious
(ahn-see-oh-soh) (ahn-see-oh-sah)
**agobiado / agobiada**                    overwhelmed
(ah-goh-bee-ah-doh) (ah-goh-bee-ah-dah)
**confundido / confundida**                confused
(kohn-foon-dee-doh) (kohn-foon-dee-dah)

¿Qué estás haciendo?
**What are you doing?**

answer with

**Estoy**
means **I am**

_estoy_
............

**comiendo**
(koh-mee-ehn-doh)

I am eating

............

**cocinando**
(koh-see-nan-doh)

I am cooking

............

**hablando por telefono**
(ah-blahn-doh pohr teh-leh-foh-noh)

I am talking on the phone

............

**escribiendo un correo electrónico**
(ehs-kree-byehn-doh oon kohr-reh-oh ehl-ehk-troh-nee-koh)

I am writing an email

............

**estudiando**
(ehs-too-dee-ahn-doh)

I am studying

............

**trabajando**
(trah-bah-hahn-doh)

I am working

............

**leyendo**
(leh-yehn-doh)

I am reading

............

**manejando**
(mah-neh-hahn-doh)

I am driving

............

**caminando**
(kah-mee-nan-doh)

I am walking

............

**sacando a mi perro a caminar**
(sah-kahn-doh ah mee pehr-roh ah kah-mee-nahr)

I am walking my dog

............

**aqui nomas relajando**
(ah-kee noh-mahs rreh-lah-han-doh)

I am just here chilling

............

**viendo netflix**
(vyehn-doh netflix)

I am watching Netflix

............

**viendo una película**
(vyehn-doh oo-nah peh-lee-koo-lah)

I am watching a movie

............

**viendo un video**
(vyehn-doh oon vee-deh-oh)

I am watching a video

............

**escuchando musica**
(ehs-koo-chahn-doh moo-see-kah)

I am listening to music

............

**practicando mi español**
(prahk-tee-kahn-doh mee ehs-pah-nyol)

I am practicing my Spanish

# Here are more examples of Spanish verbs

**maquillandome**
(mah-kee-yahn-doh-meh)

doing my makeup

**peinando**
(pay-nahn-doh)

doing my hair

**bañandome**
(bah-yahn-doh-meh)

taking a shower

**limpiando la casa**
(leem-pee-ah-n-doh lah cah-sah)

cleaning the house

**lavando la ropa**
(lah-vahn-doh lah roh-pah)

doing laundry

**recogiendo mi cuarto**
(reh-koh-he-endo mee kuar-toh)

cleaning my room

**organizando mis cosas**
(or-gahni-zan-doh mis kosas)

organizing my things

**comprando algunas cosas**
(com-pran-doh al-goo-nas kosas)

buying a couple things

**escribiendo**
(es-cree-bien-doh)

writing

**pensando**
(pen-sahn-doh)

thinking

¿Dónde Estás?
**Where are you ?**    answer with    **Estoy**
I am

| | | |
|---|---|---|
| *estoy* | **en la oficina** | I am at the office |
| | (ehn lah oh-fee-see-nah) | |
| | **en la escuela** | I am at school |
| | (ehn lah ehs-kweh-lah) | |
| | **en la casa** | I am home |
| | (ehn lah kah-sah) | |
| | **en el gymnacio** | I am at the gym |
| | (ehn ehl heem-nah-see-oh) | |
| | **en frente de ti** | I am in front of you |
| | (ehn frehn-teh deh tee) | |
| | **detras de ti** | I am behind you |
| | (deh-trahs deh tee) | |
| | **de vacaciones** | I am on vacation |
| | (deh bah-kah-see-oh nehs) | |
| | **en la playa** | I am at the beach |
| | (ehn lah plah-yah) | |
| | **de viaje** | I am on a trip |
| | (deh bee-ah-heh) | |
| | **viajando** | I am traveling |
| | (bee-ah-hahn-doh) | |
| | **en el avion** | I am on the plane |
| | (ehn ehl ah-bee-ohn) | |
| | **en mi carro / coche** | I am in my car |
| | (ehn mee kahr-roh / koh-cheh) | |
| | **en el camion** | I am on the bus |
| | (ehn ehl kah-mee-ohn) | |
| | **en la esquina** | I am at the corner |
| | (ehn lah ehs-kee-nah) | |
| | **afuera** | I am outside |
| | (ah-foo-eh-rah) | |
| | **adentro** | I am inside |
| | (ah-dehn-troh) | |

## Here are more examples of Spanish nouns

**en la tienda**                              at the store
(ehn lah tee-ehn-dah)

**en mi cuarto**                              in my room
(ehn mee koo-ahr-toh)

**en la cocina**                              in the kitchen
(ehn lah koh-see-nah)

**en el patio**                               in the backyard
(ehn ehl pah-tee-oh)

**en el jardin**                              in the garden
(ehn ehl har-deen)

**en la piscina**                             in the pool
(ehn lah pee-seen-ah)

**en el bar**                                 at the bar
(ehn ehl bahr)

**en el uber**                                in the uber
(ehn ehl uber)

**en el aeropuerto**                          at the airport
(ehn ehl ah-eh-roh-pwer-toh)

# MY NOTES

Conjugations of *estar* – to be

| PRESENT INDICATIVE FORM OF ESTAR | |
|---|---|
| I am | Estoy (es-toy) |
| You are | Estás (es-tas) |
| He / She is | Está (es-ta) |
| We are | Estamos (es-ta-mos) |
| They are | Están (es-tan) |

Conjugations of *ser* – to be

| PRESENT INDICATIVE FORM OF SER | |
|---|---|
| I am | Soy (soy) |
| You are | Eres (eres) |
| He / She is | Es (es) |
| We are | Somos (so-mos) |
| They are | Son (son) |

## Examples of *estar* in present tense.

**Estoy** muy alegre hoy.
(es-toy muy ah-le-greh oy)

**I am** very happy today.

**Estoy** comprando unas cosas

en el supermercado.

(es-toy com-pran-do oo-nas cos-as en ehl sue-per-mehr-ca-doh)

**I am** buying some things

at the grocery store.

**Estás** haciendo un buen trabajo.
(es-tas ah-see-en-doh un bwen tra-ba-ho)

**You are** doing a good job.

**Estás** bien?
(es-tas byen)

**Are you** ok?

El **está** manejando.
(ehl es-ta ma-neh-han-doh)

**He is** driving.

Ella **está** visitando a su hermana.
(eh-ya es-ta visi-tan-doh ah su ehr-ma-na)

**She is** visiting her sister.

**Estamos** a punto de llegar.
(es-tamos ah pun-toh de yeh-ghar)

**We are** about to get there.

**Estamos** todos aqui.
(es-tamos toh-dos ah-kee)

**We are** all here.

**Estan** emocionados por verte.
(es-tan eh-moh-see-oh-na-dos por ver-teh)

**They are** excited to see you.

Las llaves **estan** colgadas.
(las yah-ves es-tan col-gah-das)

The keys (**they**)**are** hanging.

# Examples of *ser* in present tense.

**Soy** una persona trabajadora.
(soy oo-na per-so-na tra-ba-ha-dora)

**I am** a hard working person.

**Soy** honesto / honesta y leal.
(soy oh-nes-toh/oh-nes-ta ee leh-al)

**I am** honest and loyal.

**Eres** gracioso / graciosa.
(eh-res grah-see-oh-so/grah-see-oh-sa)

**You are** funny.

De donde **eres**?
(de don-deh eh-res)

Where **are you** from?

**El es** musico.
(ehl es moo-see-ko)

**He is** a musician.

**Ella es** mi amiga.
(eh-ya es me ah-me-gah)

**She is** my friend.

**Somos** de California.
(so-mos deh california)

**We are** from California.

**Somos** una familia unida.
(so-mos oo-na fa-mee-lee-a oo-nee-da)

**We are** a close family.

Ellos **son** de Texas.
(eh-yos son deh texas)

**They are** from Texas.

Mis padres **son** Mexicanos.
(mees pa-dres son me-he-ca-nos)

My parents **are** Mexican.

_Tengo_ is the conjugation of the verb _tener_ - **to have** - in the present tense, in the first-person.

 The pronoun **yo** (I) is often omitted because **tengo** will always mean _I have_ weather **yo** is included or not.

# tengo  ⇨  I have
(ten-go)

**tengo una hermana**
(ten-go oo-na ehr-mah-nah)

I have a sister

**tengo un hermano**
(ten-go oon ehr-mah-noh)

I have a brother

**tengo un gemelo / una gemela**
(ten-go oon heh-meh-loh) (oo-na heh-meh-lah)

I have a male twin / female twin

**tengo pelo largo**
(ten-go peh-loh lahr-goh)

I have long hair

**tengo una cita con el doctor**
(ten-go oo-na see-tah kohn ehl dohk-tohr)

I have a doctor's appointment

**tengo fiebre**
(ten-go fee-eh-breh)

I have a fever

**tengo un dolor de cabeza**
(ten-go oon doh-lohr deh kah-veh-sah)

I have a headache

**tengo mucha tarea**
(ten-go moo-chah tah-reh-ah)

I have a lot of homework

**tengo mucho trabajo**
(ten-go moo-choh trah-bah-ho)

I have a lot of work

**tengo muchas cosas que hacer**
(ten-go moo-chahs koh-sahs keh ah-sehr)

I have a lot of things to do

**tengo un plan**
(ten-go oon plan)

I have a plan

**tengo diez mil dolares**
(ten-go dee-ehs meel doh-lah-rehs)

I have ten thousand dollars

**tengo una llamada perdida**
(ten-go oo-na yah-mah-dah pehr-dee-dah)

I have a missed call

**tengo que ir al super mercado**
(tengo keh eer ahl super mehr-kah-doh)

I have to go to the grocery store

⇨ Remember, in Spanish **tengo** can also mean **I am.**

For example:

**tengo frio / tengo calor**
(ten-go free-oh) (ten-go ka-lor)
**I am cold / I am hot**

**tengo 28 años**
(ten-go vayn-tee-oh-choh ah-nyos)

**I am 28 years old**

**tengo hambre**
(ten-go ambre)
**I am hungry**

**tengo miedo**
(ten-go me-eh-doh)

**I am scared**

**tengo sueño**
(ten-go sue-enyo)

**I am sleepy**

| | |
|---|---|
| **tenía frio** <br> (teni-ah free-oh) | **I was cold** |
| **tenía calor** <br> (teni-ah ka-lor) | **I was hot** |
| **tenía sueño** <br> (teni-ah sue-enyo) | **I was sleepy** |
| **tenía hambre** <br> (teni-ah ambre) | **I was hungry** |
| **tenía diez años** <br> (teni-ah dee-es ah-nyos) | **I was ten years old** |
| **tu tenías frio** <br> (too teni-ahs free-oh) | **you were cold** |
| **el / ella tenía calor** <br> (ehl / eh-ya teni-ah ca-lor) | **he / she was hot** |
| **teníamos sueño** <br> (teni-ah-mos sue-enyo) | **we were sleepy** |
| **ellos tenían hambre.** <br> (eh-yohs teni-ahn ambre) | **they were hungry** |

# MEXICAN SLANG

**q haces?**
¿Que haces?
**wyd?**
What are you doing?

answer with →

**Estoy**
(I am)

| slang word/phrase | slang meaning | literal translation |
| --- | --- | --- |
| **chambeando** (chahm-bay-ahn-doh) | **working** | working |
| **en el jale** (ehn ehl hah-leh) | **at work** | to pull |
| **pedo/ peda** (peh-doh) / (peh-dah) | **drunk** | fart |
| **crudo/ cruda** (croo-doh / croo-dah) | **hungover** | raw |
| **al cien** (ahl see-ehn) | **vibing / attentive** | at one hundred |

| PAST SIMPLE OF ESTAR | |
|---|---|
| I was | Estuve (es-too-veh) |
| You were | Estuviste (es-too-vees-teh) |
| He / She was | Estuvo (es-too-voh) |
| We were | Estuvimos (es-too-vee-mos) |
| They were | Estuvieron (es-too-vee-ehron) |

Conjugations of **estar** - to be

| PAST IMPERFECT OF ESTAR | |
|---|---|
| I was | Estaba (ehs-tah-bah) |
| You were | Estabas (ehs-tah-bahs) |
| He / She was | Estaba (ehs-tah-bah) |
| We were | Estabamos (ehs-tah-bah-mos) |
| They were | Estaban (ehs-tah-bahn) |

**Estuve en Chicago la semana pasada.**  **I was in Chicago last week.**
(ehs-too-veh ehn chicago lah seh-mah-nah pah-sah-dah)

**Estuve cansado/cansada toda la tarde.**  **I was tired all evening.**
(ehs-too-veh kahn-sah-doh/kahn-sah-dah toh-dah lah tahr-deh)

**Estuve esperándote.**  **I was waiting for you.**
(ehs-too-veh ehs-peh-rahn-doh-teh)

**Estuve en la feria.**  **I was at the fair.**
(ehs-too-veh ehn lah feh-ree-ah)

**Estuve de viaje en México.**  **I was on a trip to Mexico.**
(ehs-too-veh deh vee-ah-heh ehn meh-hee-koh)

**Estuve con ellos.**  **I was with them.**
(ehs-too-veh kohn eh-yohs)

Replace *estuve* with *estuviste* for **you were,** *estuvo* for **he/she was,** *estuvimos*

for **we were,** or *estuvieron* for **they were.**

**Estaba afuera cuando... (algo pasó)**
(es-tah-bah ah-foo-ehr-rah kwan-doh (al-goh pah-so))

I was outside when...
(something happened).

**Estaba jugando videojuegos.**
(es-tah-bah hoo-gahn-doh vee-deh-oh-hoo-egohs)

I was playing video games.

**Estaba estudiando para mi examen.**
(es-tah-bah es-too-dee-ahn-doh pah-rah mee eks-ah-men)

I was studying for my exam.

**Estaba hablando por teléfono y se me fue el tiempo.**
(es-tah-bah ah-blahn-doh por teh-leh-foh-noh ee
seh meh foo-eh ehl tiem-poh)

I was talking on the phone
and time flew by.

**Estaba en una junta.**
(es-tah-bah ehn oo-nah hoon-tah)

I was in a meeting.

**Estaba cocinando cuando me llamaste.**
(es-tah-bah koh-see-nahn-doh kwan-doh meh yah-mahs-teh)

I was cooking when you called me.

**Estaba en mi cuarto escuchando música.**
(es-tah-bah ehn mee kwar-toh es-koo-chahn-doh moo-zee-kah)

I was in my room listening to music.

**Estaba nervioso/a.**
(es-tah-bah nehr-byo-soh/sah)

I was nervous.

**Estaba enamorado/a.**
(es-tah-bah ehn-ah-moh-rah-doh/dah)

I was in love.

**Estaba trabajando con mi hermano.**
(es-tah-bah trah-bah-hahn-doh kon mee ehr-mah-noh)

I was working with my brother.

**Estaba enfermo/a.**
(es-tah-bah ehn-fehr-moh/mah)

I was sick.

Replace *estaba* with *estabas* for **you were,** *el/ella estaba* for **he/she was,** *estabamos* for **we were,** and *estaban* for **they were.**

| PAST SIMPLE OF SER | |
|---|---|
| I was | Fui (fwee) |
| You were | Fuiste (fwees-teh) |
| He / She was | Fue (foo-eh) |
| We were | Fuimos (fwee-mos) |
| They were | Fueron (foo-eh-ron) |

Conjugations of **ser** - to be

| PAST IMPERFECT OF SER | |
|---|---|
| I was | Era (eh-rah) |
| You were | Eras (eh-rahs) |
| He / She was | Era (eh-rah) |
| We were | Eramos (eh-rah-mos) |
| They were | Eran (eh-rahn) |

**Fui miembro de esa organización.**
(fwee mee-ehm-broh deh eh-sah ohr-gah-nee-sah-cion)

I was a member of that organization.

**Fui invitado/a a su fiesta de cumpleaños.**
(fwee een-vee-tah-doh ah sue fee-es-tah deh koom-pleh-ahn-yohs)

I was invited to their birthday party.

**Fui maletero en ese hotel.**
(fwee mah-leh-teh-roh ehn eh-seh oh-tehl)

I was a porter at that hotel.

**Fui el mejor candidato.**
(fwee ehl meh-hor kahn-dee-dah-toh)

I was the best candidate. male

**Fui la mejor candidata.**
(fwee lah meh-hor kahn-dee-dah-tah)

I was the best candidate. female

**Fui muy cruel contigo.**
(fwee muy kroo-ehl kon-tee-goh)

I was very cruel to you.

**Fui muy cortante con el/ella.**
(fwee muy kohr-tahn-teh kon ehl/eh-yah)

I was very short with him/her.

**Era un estudiante.**
(eh-rah oon es-too-dyahn-teh)

I/he/she was a student

**Era introvertido/a.**
(eh-rah een-troh-vehr-tee-doh/dah)

I/he/she was an introvert

**Era extrovertido/a.**
(eh-rah eks-troh-vehr-tee-doh/dah)

I/he/she was an extrovert

**Era tímido/a.**
(eh-rah tee-mee-doh/dah)

I/he/she was shy

**Era ingenuo/a.**
(eh-rah een-hen-oo-oh/ah)

I/he/she was naive

# MY NOTES

# Planeador Semanal

Weekly planner

## Semana de:
week of:

| |
|---|

**lunes**
Monday

**martes**
Tuesday

**miercoles**
Wednesday

**jueves**
Thursday

**viernes**
Friday

**sabado**
Saturday

**domingo**
Sunday

## Cosas que hacer
things to do

## Recordatorio
reminder

Notes
**Notas**

55

# A noun is a person, place or thing

In Spanish all nouns are either
*masculine* or *feminine*

| el, la, los, las | means | the |
|---|---|---|

**Most nouns that end in "o" are masculine.
Therefore, the difinite article will be "el"**

Singular nouns that are masculine

**el concierto** (ehl kohn-see-ehr-toh) — **the concert**

**el baño** (ehl bah-nyoh) — **the bathroom**

**el niño** (ehl nee-nyoh) — **the boy**

**el muchacho** (ehl moo-chah-choh) — **the guy**

**el rancho** (ehl rahn-choh) — **the ranch**

**el telefono** (ehl teh-leh-foh-noh) — **the phone**

**el cuaderno** (ehl kwah-dehr-noh) — **the notebook**

**el libro** (ehl lee-broh) — **the book**

**el dinero** (ehl dee-neh-roh) — **the money**

**el banco** (ehl bahn-koh) — **the bank**

**el coche** (ehl koh-cheh) — **the car**

**el perro** (ehl pehr-roh) — **the dog**

**el gato** (ehl gah-toh) — **the cat**

**el caballo** (ehl kah-bah-yoh) — **the horse**

**el vino** (ehl vee-noh) — **the wine**

**el espejo** (ehl ehs-peh-ho) — **the mirror**

**el plato** (ehl plah-toh) — **the plate**

**el vaso** (ehl vah-soh) — **the cup**

## Other singular nouns that do not end in "o" but are still masculine.

| | |
|---|---|
| **el chisme** (ehl cheez-meh) | the gossip |
| **el hombre** (ehl ohm-breh) | the man |
| **el celular** (ehl seh-loo-lahr) | the cellphone |
| **el cargador** (ehl kahr-gah-dohr) | the charger |
| **el animal** (ehl ah-nee-mahl) | the animal |
| **el tenedor** (ehl teh-neh-dohr) | the fork |
| **el doctor** (ehl dohk-tor) | the doctor (male) |
| **el hospital** (ehl ohs-pee-tahl) | the hospital |
| **el hotel** (ehl oh-tehl) | the hotel |
| **el café** (ehl kah-feh) | the coffee |
| **el pan** (ehl pahn) | the bread |
| **el tamal** (ehl tah-mahl) | the tamale |
| **el suéter** (ehl sweh-tehr) | the sweater |
| **el árbol** (ehl ahr-bohl) | the tree |
| **el sol** (ehl sol) | the sun |
| **el planeta** (ehl plah-neh-tah) | the planet |
| **el mapa** (ehl mah-pah) | the map |
| **el clima** (ehl clee-mah) | the weather |
| **el programa** (ehl pro-gra-mah) | the program |
| **el sistema** (ehl see-steh-mah) | the system |
| **el idioma** (ehl ee-dee-ohma) | the language |
| **el problema** (ehl proh-bleh-mah) | the problem |
| **el lapiz** (ehl lah-pees) | the pencil |
| **el dia** (ehl dee-ah) | the day |
| **el mes** (ehl mehs) | the month |

# Changing singular nouns to plural nouns.

If a <u>masculine</u> noun ends in a vowel,
then

## add **-s** to make it plural

**el** $\xrightarrow{\text{turns to}}$ **los**

(ehl)  (lohs)

<u>Singular nouns that are masculine</u>

**el dia**    the day
(ehl dee-ah)

**el libro**    the book
(ehl lee-broh)

**el gato**    the cat
(ehl gah-toh)

**el carro**    the car
(ehl ka-rroh)

**el zapato**    the shoe
(ehl sah-pah-toh)

**el cuarto**    the room
(ehl kwar-toh)

**el cepillo**    the brush
(ehl seh-pee-yoh)

**el cuchillo**    the knife
(ehl koo-chee-yoh)

**el niño**    the boy
(ehl nee-nyoh)

**el muchacho**    the guy
(ehl moo-cha-choh)

**el problema**    the problem
(ehl proh-bleh-mah)

**el planeta**    the planet
(ehl plah-neh-tah)

<u>Plural nouns that are masculine</u>

**los dias**    the days
(los dee-ahs)

**los libros**    the books
(los lee-brohs)

**los gatos**    the cats
(los gah-tohs)

**los carros**    the cars
(los ka-rrohs)

**los zapatos**    the shoes
(los sah-pah-tohs)

**los cuartos**    the rooms
(ehl kwar-toh)

**los cepillos**    the brushes
(los seh-pee-yohs)

**los cuchillos**    the knifes
(los koo-chee-yohs)

**los niños**    the boys
(los nyee-nyohs)

**los muchachos**    the guys
(los moo-cha-chohs)

**los problemas**    the problems
(los proh-bleh-mas)

**los planetas**    the planets
(los plah-neh-tahs)

# Most nouns that end in "a" are feminine.
# Therefore, the definite article will be "la"

| | |
|---|---|
| **la silla**<br>(la see-yah) | the chair |
| **la mesa**<br>(la meh-sah) | the table |
| **la esquina**<br>(la ehs-kee-nah) | the corner |
| **la cara**<br>(la kah-rah) | the face |
| **la crema**<br>(la kreh-mah) | the cream / the lotion |
| **la parrilla**<br>(la pah-ree-yah) | the grill |
| **la computadora**<br>(la kohm-poo-tah-doh-rah) | the computer |
| **la granja**<br>(la grahn-hah) | the barn |
| **la niña**<br>(la nee-nyah) | the little girl |
| **la muchacha**<br>(la moo-chah-chah) | the girl, young lady |
| **la cobija**<br>(la koh-bee-hah) | the blanket |
| **la camisa**<br>(la kah-mee-sah) | the shirt |
| **la cama**<br>(la kah-mah) | the bed |
| **la cerveza**<br>(la sehr-veh-sah) | the beer |
| **la persona**<br>(la pehr-soh-nah) | the person |
| **la tienda**<br>(la tee-ehn-dah) | the store |
| **la bolsa**<br>(la bohl-sah) | the bag |

**Other singular nouns that do not end in "a" but are still feminine.**

| | |
|---|---|
| **la mano** <br> (la mah-no) | the hand |
| **la foto** <br> (la foh-toh) | the picture |
| **la luz** <br> (la loose) | the light |
| **la llave** <br> (lah yah-veh) | the key |
| **la gente** <br> (la hen-teh) | the people |
| **la noche** <br> (la no-cheh) | the night |
| **la tarde** <br> (la tar-deh) | the afternoon / evening |
| **la nube** <br> (la noo-beh) | the cloud |
| **la miel** <br> (la mee-ehl) | the honey |
| **la carne** <br> (la kahr-neh) | the meat |
| **la moto** <br> (la moh-toh) | the motorcycle |
| **la clase** <br> (la klah-seh) | the class |
| **la sal** <br> (la sahl) | the salt |
| **la conversacion** <br> (la kohn-vehr-sah-syohn) | the conversation |
| **la flor** <br> (la flor) | the flower |
| **la mujer** <br> (la moo-hehr) | the women |
| **la calle** <br> (la kah-yeh) | the street |
| **la razon** <br> (la rah-sohn) | the reason |
| **la piel** <br> (la pee-ehl) | the skin |
| **la clave** <br> (la klah-veh) | the code |
| **la ciudad** <br> (la see-oo-dahd) | the city |
| **la verdad** <br> (la vehr-dahd) | the truth |

# Changing singular nouns to plural nouns.

### If a <u>feminine</u> noun ends in a vowel, then

## add **-s** to make it plural

## la turns to → las

Singular nouns that are feminine

**la camioneta** — the truck
(la kah-mee-oh-neh-tah)

**la playa** — the beach
(la plah-yah)

**la foto** — the picture
(la foh-toh)

**la mano** — the hand
(la mah-no)

**la pulsera** — the bracelet
(la pool-seh-rah)

**la cadena** — the necklace
(la kah-deh-nah)

**la puerta** — the door
(la pwehr-tah)

**la pelicula** — the movie
(la peh-lee-koo-lah)

**la rola(cancion)** — the song
(la row-la) (la kahn-syohn)

**la uña** — the nail
(la oo-nyah)

**la botella** — the bottle
(la boh-teh-yah)

**la tienda** — the store
(la tee-ehn-dah)

Plural nouns that are feminine

**las camionetas** — the trucks
(las kah-mee-oh-neh-tahs)

**las playas** — the beaches
(las plah-yahs)

**las fotos** — the pictures
(las foh-tohs)

**las manos** — the hands
(las mah-nohs)

**las pulseras** — the bracelets
(las pool-seh-rahs)

**las cadenas** — the necklaces
(las kah-deh-nahs)

**las puertas** — the doors
(las pwehr-tahs)

**las peliculas** — the movies
(las peh-lee-koo-lahs)

**las rolas(canciones)** — the songs
(las row-las) (las kahn-syohn-es)

**las uñas** — the nails
(las oon-nyahs)

**las botellas** — the bottles
(las boh-teh-yahs)

**las tiendas** — the stores
(las tee-ehn-das)

# Changing singular nouns to plural nouns.

### If a noun ends in a <u>consonant</u>

## add **-es** to make it plural.

| | | | |
|---|---|---|---|
| **la ciudad**<br>(la see-oo-dahd) | the city | **las ciudades**<br>(las see-oo-dahd-es) | the cities |
| **la conversación**<br>(la kohn-vehr-sah-syohn) | the conversation | **las conversaciónes**<br>(las kohn-vehr-sah-syohn-es) | the conversations |
| **la luz**<br>(la loose) | the light | **las luces**<br>(las loose-es) | the lights |
| **la razon**<br>(la rah-sohn) | the reason | **las razones**<br>(las rah-sohn-es) | the reasons |
| **el color**<br>(ehl coh-lor) | the color | **los colores**<br>(los coh-lor-es) | the colors |
| **el tamal**<br>(ehl tah-mahl) | the tamale | **los tamales**<br>(los tah-mahl-es) | the tamales |
| **el animal**<br>(ehl ah-nee-mahl) | the animal | **los animales**<br>(los ah-nee-mahl-es) | the animals |
| **el cargador**<br>(ehl kahr-gah-dor) | the charger | **los cargadores**<br>(los kahr-gah-dor-es) | the chargers |
| **el arbol**<br>(ehl ahr-bohl) | the tree | **los arboles**<br>(los ahr-bohl-es) | the trees |
| **el marcador**<br>(ehl mark-ah-dor) | the marker | **los marcadores**<br>(los mark-ah-dor-es) | the markers |
| **la mujer**<br>(la moo-hehr) | the woman | **las mujeres**<br>(las moo-hehr-es) | the women |
| **la ley**<br>(la lei) | the law | **las leyes**<br>(las lei-es) | the laws |
| **el hotel**<br>(ehl oh-tel) | the hotel | **los hoteles**<br>(los oh-tel-es) | the hotels |
| **el rey**<br>(ehl ray) | the king | **los reyes**<br>(los ray-es) | the kings |
| **el canal**<br>(ehl ka-nahl) | the channel | **los canales**<br>(los ka-nahl-es) | the channels |
| **la imagen**<br>(la eema-hen) | the image | **las imagenes**<br>(las eema-hen-es) | the images |
| **la flor**<br>(la flor) | the flower | **las flores**<br>(las flor-es) | the flowers |
| **el camion**<br>(ehl kah-mee-ohn) | the bus | **los camiones**<br>(los kah-mee-ohn-es) | the buses |

# MY NOTES

## Subject pronouns

The subject pronouns represent the subject in the sentence.

**Yo hablo español.**
(yoh ahblo ehs-pah-nyohl)

I speak Spanish.

**Yo quiero ir contigo.**
(yoh kee-ehr-oh eer kohn-tee-goh)

I want to go with you.

**Yo no sé.**
(yoh no seh)

I don't know.

**Yo te invito.**
(yoh teh in-vee-toh)

My treat (I'll invite you)

**Yo no quiero.**
(yoh no kee-ehr-oh)

I don't want to.

**Yo no dije eso.**
(yoh no dee-heh es-oh)

I didn't say that.

**Yo te recojo.**
(yoh teh reh-koh-hoh)

I will pick you up.

**¿Y yo que?**
(ee yoh keh)

What about me?

**Yo lo hice.**
(yoh loh ee-seh)

I did it.

**¡Yo!**
(yoh)

Me!

| Singular | | |
|---|---|---|
| yo (yoh) | informal | I |
| tú (too) | | you |
| usted (oos-tehd) | formal | you |
| él (ehl) | | he |
| ella (eh-yah) | | she |

*Tú* and *usted* both translate to *you*.

**Tú** is more *laidback*. Use it when speaking to family, friends, or a child.

**Usted** is more formal. It's more polite. Use it when speaking to a stranger, an elderly person, or someone of authority like a boss or teacher.

**¿Tu que quieres?**
(too keh kee-ehr-es)

**¿Usted que va a querer?**
(oos-tehd keh vah ah keh-rehr)

What do you want?

**¿Hola, como estas?**
(oh-lah, koh-moh es-tahs)

**¿Hola, como esta?**
(oh-lah, koh-moh es-tah)

Hello, how are you?

**¿Me puedes dar un consejo?**
(meh pweh-dehs dar oon kohn-seh-ho)

**¿Me puede dar un consejo?**
(meh pweh-deh dar oon kohn-seh-ho)

Can you give me advice?

**Eres muy inteligente.**
(ehr-ehs muy een-teh-lee-hen-teh)

**Usted es muy inteligente.**
(oos-tehd ehs mwee in-teh-lee-hen-teh)

You are very smart.

**Te agradesco tu ayuda.**
(teh ah-grah-dehs-koh too ah-yoo-dah)

**Le agradesco su ayuda.**
(leh ah-grah-dehs-koh soo ah-yoo-dah)

I'm thankful for your help.

**Cual es tu numero?**
(kwahl ehs too noo-meh-roh)

**¿Cual es su numero?**
(kwahl ehs sue noo-meh-roh)

What's your number?

**¿Como te puedo ayudar?**
(koh-moh teh pweh-do ah-yoo-dar)

**¿Como le puedo ayudar?**
(koh-moh leh pweh-do ah-yoo-dar)

How can I help you?

**Estoy pensando en ti.**
(es-toy pehn-sahn-doh ehn tee)

**Estoy pensando en usted.**
(ehs-toy pehn-sahn-doh en oos-tehd)

I'm thinking of you.

**¿Como te llamas?**
(koh-moh teh yah-mahs)

**¿Como se llama?**
(koh-moh seh yah-mah)

What's your name?

## Subject pronouns

The subject pronouns represent the subject in the sentence.

**Él dijo eso.**        He said that.
(ehl dee-ho es-oh)

**Él fue a Guanajuato la semana pasada.**    He went to Guanajuato last week.
(ehl fweh ah goo-ana-hoo-ahto lah seh-mah-nah pah-sah-dah)

**Él me va a regojer.**        He is going to pick me up.
(ehl meh vah ah reh-koh-hehr)

**Él tiene una esposa/novia.**      He has a wife/girlfriend.
(ehl tee-ehn-eh oo-nah es-poh-sah/no-vee-ah)

**¿Cuantos años tiene él?**      How old is he?
(kwahn-tohs ah-nyohs tee-ehn-eh ehl)

**Ella es/esta muy bonita.**      She is very pretty.
(eh-yah ehs/ehs-tah mwee boh-nee-tah)

**¿Quien es ella?**      Who is she?
(kee-ehn es eh-yah)

**Ella es la patrona.**      She is the boss.
(eh-yah ehs lah pah-troh-nah)

**A ella le gusta hablar mucho.**      She likes to talk a lot.
(ah eh-yah leh goos-tah ah-blahr moo-choh)

**Ella es mi madre.**      She is my mother.
(eh-yah ehs mee mah-dreh)

**Yo** = I, the subject of a sentence. Yo no quiero ir. I don't want to go.
(yo)

**Me** = I or to me, this is an object pronoun or it can be a reflexive pronoun.
(meh)

**Mí (with accent mark)** = me, personal pronoun.
(mee)

**Mi** = my, is a possessive pronoun.   ⟶   **mi casa** (my house)
(mee)                               **mi libro** (my book)

                                          **mis amigos** (my friends)

## Plural

| | | |
|---|---|---|
| nosotros (noh-soh-tros) | we | |
| ellos (eh-yohs) | they | |
| ellas (eh-yas) | they | |
| ustedes (oos-teh-dehs) | you - all | |

*Ellos* and *nosotros* are used for a group of men or a group of men and women.
*Ellas* and *nosotras* are exclusively used when describing a group of women.

**Nosotros estamos en el mismo equipo.**
(no-soh-trohs es-tah-mohs en ehl mee-smo eh-kee-poh)
We are on the same team.

**Nosotras tenemos mucha tarea.**
(noh-soh-trahs teh-neh-mohs moo-chah tah-reh-ah)
We (females) have a lot of homework.

**¿Quien va ir? Nada más nosotros.**
(kee-ehn vah ah eer? nah-dah mahs noh-soh-trohs)
Who is going? Just us (we)

**Nosotros vivimos en el rancho.**
(noh-soh-trohs vee-vee-mohs ehn ehl rahn-choh)
We live on the farm/ranch.

**Nosotras estamos contentas.**
(noh-soh-trahs ehs-tah-mohs kohn-tehn-tahs)
We (females) are happy.


**Ellos son bien lindos.**
(eh-yohs sohn byehn leen-dohs)
They are so cute/sweet.

**Ellos están aqui.**
(eh-yohs es-tahn ah-kee)
They are here.

**¿Quienes son ellos?**
(kee-en-es sohn eh-yohs)
Who are they?

**Ellos son chingones para trabajar.**
(eh-yohs sohn cheen-goh-nehs pah-rah trah-bah-hahr)
They are fucking beasts at work.

**Me caen muy bien ellos.**
(meh kah-ehn muy byehn eh-yohs)
I really like them.


**Ellas fueron a desayunar.**
(eh-yahs fweh-rohn ah deh-sah-yoo-nahr)
They(female) went to get breakfast.

**Ellas son mejores amigas.**
(eh-yahs sohn meh-ho-rehs ah-mee-gahs)
They(female) are besties - best friends.

**Quiero hablar con ellas.**
(kee-ehr-oh ah-blahr kohn eh-yahs)
I want to speak with them(female).

**¿Donde están ellas?**
(dohn-deh ehs-tahn eh-yahs)
Where are they(female)?

**Ellas quieren ganar.**
(eh-yahs kee-ehr-ehn gah-nahr)
They(female) want to win.


**¿Qué tal están ustedes hoy?**
(keh tahl ehs-tahn oos-teh-dehs oy)
How are you all doing today?

**Ustedes son muy amables.**
(oos-teh-dehs sohn mwee ah-mah-blehs)
You all are very kind.

**¿Pueden ustedes ayudarme con esto?**
(pweh-dehn oos-teh-dehs ah-yoo-dahr-meh kohn ehs-toh)
Can you all help me with this?

# Spanish verbs and their conjugation in the present tense

ser (to be):

    soy (I am)

    eres (you are [informal])

    es (he/she/it is)

    somos (we are)

    son (they are)

estar (to be):

    estoy (I am)

    estás (you are [informal])

    está (he/she/it is)

    estamos (we are)

    están (they are)

tener (to have):

    tengo (I have)

    tienes (you have [informal])

    tiene (he/she/it has)

    tenemos (we have)

    tienen (they have)

hacer (to do/make):

    hago (I do/make)

    haces (you do/make [informal])

    hace (he/she/it does/makes)

    hacemos (we do/make)

    hacen (they do/make)

ir (to go):

    voy (I go)

    vas (you go [informal])

    va (he/she/it goes)

    vamos (we go)

    van (they go)

comprar (to buy):

    compro (I buy)

    compras (you buy [informal])

    compra (he/she/it buys)

    compramos (we buy)

    compran (they buy)

escribir (to write):

    escribes (you write [informal])

    escribe (he/she/it writes)

    escribimos (we write)

    escriben (they write)

hablar (to speak):

    hablo (I speak)

    hablas (you speak [informal])

    habla (he/she/it speaks)

    hablamos (we speak)

    hablan (they speak)

vivir (to live):

    vivo (I live)

    vives (you live [informal])

    vive (he/she/it lives)

    vivimos (we live)

    viven (they live)

decir (to say):

    digo (I say)

    dices (you say [informal])

    dice (he/she/it says)

    decimos (we say)

    dicen (they say)

ver (to see):

    veo (I see)

    ves (you see [informal])

    ve (he/she/it sees)

    vemos (we see)

    ven (they see)

# Spanish verbs and their conjugation in the present tense

oír (to hear):
- oigo (I hear)
- oyes (you hear [informal])
- oye (he/she/it hears)
- oímos (we hear)
- oyen (they hear)

poder (to be able to):
- puedo (I can)
- puedes (you can [informal])
- puede (he/she/it can)
- podemos (we can)
- pueden (they can)

saber (to know):
- yo sé (I know)
- sabes (you know [informal])
- sabe (he/she/it knows)
- sabemos (we know)
- saben (they know)

querer (to want):
- quiero (I want)
- quieres (you want [informal])
- quiere (he/she/it wants)
- queremos (we want)
- quieren (they want)

conocer (to know [a person or a place]):
- conozco (I know)
- conoces (you know [informal])
- conoce (he/she/it knows)
- conocemos (we know)
- conocen (they know)

viajar (to travel):
- viajo (I travel)
- viajas (you travel [informal])
- viaja (he/she/it travels)
- viajamos (we travel)
- viajan (they travel)

estudiar (to study):
- estudio (I study)
- estudias (you study [informal])
- estudia (he/she/it studies)
- estudiamos (we study)
- estudian (they study)

llevar (to carry):
- llevo (I carry)
- llevas (you carry [informal])
- lleva (he/she/it carries)
- llevamos (we carry)
- llevan (they carry)

traer (to bring):
- traigo (I bring)
- traes (you bring [informal])
- trae (he/she/it brings)
- traemos (we bring)
- traen (they bring)

dar (to give):
- doy (I give)
- das (you give [informal])
- da (he/she/it gives)
- damos (we give)
- dan (they give)

salir (to leave):
- salgo (I leave)
- sales (you leave [informal])
- sale (he/she/it leaves)
- salimos (we leave)
- salen (they leave)

entrar (to enter):
- entro (I enter)
- entras (you enter [informal])
- entra (he/she/it enters)
- entramos (we enter)

## Spanish verbs and their conjugation in the past tense

hacer (to do/make):

    hice (I did/made)

    hiciste (you did/made [informal])

    hizo (he/she/it did/made)

    hicimos (we did/made)

    hicieron (they did/made)

hacer (to do/make):

    hacía (I was doing/making)

    hacías (you were doing/making [informal])

    hacía (he/she/it was doing/making)

    hacíamos (we were doing/making)

tener (to have):

    tuve (I had)

    tuviste (you had [informal])

    tuvo (he/she/it had)

    tuvimos (we had)

    tuvieron (they had)

decir (to say):

    dije (I said)

    dijiste (you said [informal])

    dijo (he/she/it said)

    dijimos (we said)

    dijeron (they said)

poder (to be able to):

    pude (I was able to)

    pudiste (you were able to [informal])

    pudo (he/she/it was able to)

    pudimos (we were able to)

    pudieron (they were able to)

querer (to want):

    quise (I wanted)

    quisiste (you wanted [informal])

    quiso (he/she/it wanted)

    quisimos (we wanted)

    quisieron (they wanted)

saber (to know [information]):

    supe (I knew [info])

    supiste (you knew [info] [informal])

    supo (he/she/it knew [info])

    supimos (we knew [info])

    supieron (they knew [info])

poner (to put):

    puse (I put)

    pusiste (you put [informal])

    puso (he/she/it put)

    pusimos (we put)

    pusieron (they put)

llevar (to take [to carry]):

    llevé (I took)

    llevaste (you took [informal])

    llevó (he/she/it took)

    llevamos (we took)

    llevaron (they carried)

comer (to eat):

    comí (I ate)

    comiste (you ate [informal])

    comió (he/she/it ate)

    comimos (we ate)

    comieron (they ate)

ver (to see):

    vi (I saw)

    viste (you saw [informal])

    vio (he/she/it saw)

    vimos (we saw)

    vieron (they saw)

ir (to go):

    fui (I went)

    fuiste (you went [informal])

    fue (he/she/it went)

    fuimos (we went)

    fueron (they went)

## Spanish verbs and their conjugation in the past tense

escribir (to write):
- escribí (I wrote)
- escribiste (you wrote [informal])
- escribió (he/she/it wrote)
- escribimos (we wrote)
- escribieron (they wrote)

estudiar (to study):
- estudié (I studied)
- estudiaste (you studied [informal])
- estudió (he/she/it studied)
- estudiamos (we studied)
- estudiaron (they studied)

conocer (to know [a person or a place]):
- conocí (I met/knew)
- conociste (you met/knew [informal])
- conoció (he/she/it met/knew)
- conocimos (we met/knew)
- conocieron (they met/knew)

pedir (to ask for):
- pedí (I asked for)
- pediste (you asked for [informal])
- pidió (he/she/it asked for)
- pedimos (we asked for)
- pidieron (they asked for)

comprar (to buy):
- compré (I bought)
- compraste (you bought [informal])
- compró (he/she/it bought)
- compramos (we bought)
- compraron (they bought)

traer (to bring):
- traje (I brought)
- trajiste (you brought [informal])
- trajo (he/she/it brought)
- trajimos (we brought)
- trajeron (they brought)

dar (to give):
- di (I gave)
- diste (you gave [informal])
- dio (he/she/it gave)
- dimos (we gave)
- dieron (they gave)

salir (to leave):
- salí (I left)
- saliste (you left [informal])
- salió (he/she/it left)
- salimos (we left)
- salieron (they left)

entrar (to enter):
- entré (I entered)
- entraste (you entered [informal])
- entró (he/she/it entered)
- entramos (we entered)
- entraron (they entered)

## Spanish verbs and their conjugation in the future tense

venir (to come):

    voy a venir (I will come)

    vas a venir (you will come [informal])

    va a venir (he/she/it will come)

    vamos a venir (we will come)

    van a venir (they will come)

ir (to go):

    voy a ir (I will go)

    vas a ir (you will go [informal])

    va a ir (he/she/it will go)

    vamos a ir (we will go)

    van a ir (they will go)

decir (to say):

    voy a decir (I will say)

    vas a decir (you will say [informal])

    va a decir (he/she/it will say)

    vamos a decir (we will say)

    van a decir (they will say)

ver (to see):

    voy a ver (I will see)

    vas a ver (you will see [informal])

    va a ver (he/she/it will see)

    vamos a ver (we will see)

    van a ver (they will see)

oír (to hear):

    voy a oír (I will hear)

    vas a oír (you will hear [informal])

    va a oír (he/she/it will hear)

    vamos a oír (we will hear)

    van a oír (they will hear)

poder (to be able to):

    voy a poder (I will be able to)

    vas a poder (you will be able to [informal])

    va a poder (he/she/it will be able to)

    vamos a poder (we will be able to)

    van a poder (they will be able to)

querer (to want):

    voy a querer (I will want)

    vas a querer (you will want [informal])

    va a querer (he/she/it will want)

    vamos a querer (we will want)

    van a querer (they will want)

saber (to know [information]):

    voy a saber (I will know [information])

    vas a saber (you will know [information] [informal])

    va a saber (he/she/it will know [information])

    vamos a saber (we will know [information])

    van a saber (they will know [information])

dar (to give):

    voy a dar (I will give)

    vas a dar (you will give [singular informal])

    va a dar (he/she/it will give)

    vamos a dar (we will give)

    van a dar (they will give)

## Spanish verbs and their conjugation in the future tense

poner (to put):
- voy a poner (I will put)
- vas a poner (you will put [informal])
- va a poner (he/she/it will put)
- vamos a poner (we will put)
- van a poner (they will put)

llevar (to carry):
- voy a llevar (I will carry)
- vas a llevar (you will carry [informal])
- va a llevar (he/she/it will carry)
- vamos a llevar (we will carry)
- van a llevar (they will carry)

traer (to bring):
- voy a traer (I will bring)
- vas a traer (you will bring [informal])
- va a traer (he/she/it will bring)
- vamos a traer (we will bring)
- van a traer (they will bring)

salir (to exit/go out):
- voy a salir (I will exit/go out)
- vas a salir (you will exit/go out [informal])
- va a salir (he/she/it will exit/go out)
- vamos a salir (we will exit/go out)
- van a salir (they will exit/go out)

entrar (to enter):
- voy a entrar (I will enter)
- vas a entrar (you will enter [informal])
- va a entrar (he/she/it will enter)
- vamos a entrar (we will enter)
- van a entrar (they will enter)

encontrar (to find):
- voy a encontrar (I will find)
- vas a encontrar (you will find [informal])
- va a encontrar (he/she/it will find)
- vamos a encontrar (we will find)
- van a encontrar (they will find)

hablar (to speak):
- voy a hablar (I will speak)
- vas a hablar (you will speak [informal])
- va a hablar (he/she/it will speak)
- vamos a hablar (we will speak)
- van a hablar (they will speak)

comer (to eat):
- voy a comer (I will eat)
- vas a comer (you will eat [informal])
- va a comer (he/she/it will eat)
- vamos a comer (we will eat)
- van a comer (they will eat)

beber (to drink):
- voy a beber (I will drink)
- vas a beber (you will drink)
- va a beber (he/she/it will drink)
- vamos a beber (we will drink)
- van a beber (they will drink)

escribir (to write):
- voy a escribir (I will write)
- vas a escribir (you will write [informal])
- va a escribir (he/she/it will write)
- vamos a escribir (we will write)
- van a escribir (they will write)

leer (to read):
- voy a leer (I will read)
- vas a leer (you will read [informal])
- va a leer (he/she/it will read)
- vamos a leer (we will read)
- van a leer (they will read)

# 110 Spanish nouns

**Casa (house)**
(kah-sah)
**Perro (dog)**
(peh-rrro)
**Gente (people)**
(hen-teh)
**Tiempo (time)**
(tee-em-poh)
**Dinero (money)**
(dee-neh-roh)
**Trabajo (work)**
(tra-bah-ho)
**Amigo (friend)**
(ah-mee-go)
**Familia (family)**
(fah-mee-lee-ah)
**Escuela (school)**
(es-kwe-la)
**Comida (food)**
(co-mee-da)
**Agua (water)**
(ah-gwah)
**Cielo (sky)**
(see-eh-lo)
**Tierra (earth)**
(tee-eh-rra)
**Silla (chair)**
(see-ya)
**Ciudad (city)**
(see-oo-dahd)
**Libreria (library)**
(lee-breh-ree-ah)
**Universidad (university)**
(ooni-vehr-see-dahd)
**Hospital (hospital)**
(os-pee-tahl)
**Carro (car)**
(kah-rro)
**Computadora (computer)**
(kohm-poo-tah-doh-rah)
**Teléfono (telephone)**
(teh-leh-foh-no)
**Cama (bed)**
(kah-mah)
**Estrella (star)**
(es-treh-ya)

**Naturaleza (nature)**
(nah-too-rah-leh-sa)
**Paz (peace)**
(pahs)
**Cultura (culture)**
(kool-too-rah)
**Belleza (beauty)**
(be-yeh-sa)
**Mar (sea)**
(mahr)
**Montaña (mountain)**
(mohn-tah-nyah)
**Parque (park)**
(pahr-keh)
**Tienda (store)**
(tee-ehn-dah)
**Biblioteca (library)**
(blee-blee-oh-teh-ka)
**Cine (cinema)**
(seen-eh)
**Museo (museum)**
(moo-seh-oh)
**Restaurante (restaurant)**
(res-tau-rahn-teh)
**Aeropuerto (airport)**
(ah-eh-ro-poo-er-toh)

**Playa (beach)**
(play-ah)
**Hotel (hotel)**
(oh-tel)
**Bar (bar)**
(bahr)
**Paisaje (landscape)**
(pie-sah-he)
**Musica (music)**
(moo-see-kah)
**Arte (art)**
(ahr-te)
**Deporte (sport)**
(de-por-te)
**Pelicula (movie)**
(pe-lee-koo-lah)
**Teatro (theater)**
(te-ah-tro)
**Cancion (song)**
(kahn-see-on)

**Baño (bathroom)**
(bahn-yo)
**Cuarto (room)**
(kwahr-to)
**Jardín (garden)**
(hahr-deen)
**Oficina (office)**
(oh-fee-see-nah)
**Negocio (business)**
(ne-goh-see-oh)
**Piso (floor)**
(pee-so)
**Edificio (building)**
(ed-ee-fee-see-oh)
**Calle (street)**
(kah-ye)
**Sillón (couch)**
(see-yon)
**Pais (country)**
(pah-yees)
**Continente (continent)**
(kon-teen-te)
**Lenguaje (language)**
(len-gwah-he)
**Literatura (literature)**
(lee-te-rah-too-rah)
**Tecnología (technology)**
(tehk-no-loh-he-ah)
**Mundo (world)**
(moon-doh)
**Ciencia (science)**
(see-ehn-see-ah)
**Educación (education)**
(ed-oo-kah-see-on)
**Bicicleta (bicycle)**
(bee-see-cle-tah)
**Transporte (transportation)**
(trans-por-te)
**Energía (energy)**
(eh-ner-hee-ah)
**Energia solar (solar energy)**
(eh-ner-hee-ah so-lar)
**Política (politics)**
(poh-lee-tee-kah)
**Economía (economy)**
(eh-koh-noh-mee-ah)

# 110 Spanish nouns

**Sociedad (society)**
(soh-see-eh-dahd)

**Historia (history)**
(ee-sto-ree-ah)

**Geografía (geography)**
(he-oh-grah-fee-ah)

**Religión (religion)**
(reh-lee-he-on)

**Filosofía (philosophy)**
(fee-loh-soh-fee-ah)

**Psicología (psychology)**
(see-koh-loh-he-ah)

**Medio Ambiente (environment)**
(meh-dee-oh am-bee-ehn-te)

**Agricultura (agriculture)**
(ah-gree-kool-too-rah)

**Terreno (plot of land)**
(teh-rre-no)

**Industria (industry)**
(een-doo-stree-ah)

**Comercio (commerce)**
(kohm-ehr-see-oh)

**Comunicaciones (communications)**
(koh-moo-nee-kah-see-on-es)

**Matemáticas (mathematics)**
(mah-teh-mah-tee-kahs)

**Física (physics)**
(fee-see-kah)

**Química (chemistry)**
(keh-mee-kah)

**Biología (biology)**
(bee-oh-loh-he-ah)

**Astronomía (astronomy)**
(ahs-troh-noh-mee-ah)

**Arqueología (archeology)**
(ahr-keh-oh-loh-he-ah)

**Antropología (anthropology)**
(ahn-troh-poh-loh-he-ah)

**Geología (geology)**
(he-oh-loh-he-ah)

**Arquitectura (architecture)**
(ahr-kee-tehk-too-rah)

**Urbanismo (urbanism)**
(oor-bahn-ee-zmo)

**Moda (fashion)**
(moh-dah)

**Cocina (kitchen)**
(koh-see-nah)

**Jardinería (gardening)**
(hahr-dee-neh-ree-ah)

**Decoración (decoration)**
(deh-koh-rah-see-on)

**Fotografía (photography)**
(foh-toh-grah-fee-ah)

**Cine (film)**
(seen-eh)

**Televisión (television)**
(teh-leh-bee-see-on)

**Radio (radio)**
(rah-dee-oh)

**Periodismo (journalism)**
(peh-ree-oh-dee-zmoh)

**Publicidad (advertising)**
(poo-blee-see-dahd)

**Marketing (marketing)**
(mahr-keh-teeng)

**Negocios (business)**
(neh-goh-see-ohs)

**Finanzas (finance)**
(fee-nahn-zahs)

**Administración (administration)**
(ahd-mee-nee-strah-see-on)

**Recursos humanos (human resources)**
(reh-koor-sohs oo-mah-nohs)

**Seguros (insurance)**
(seh-gw-rohs)

**Cuenta (account)**
(koo-enta)

**Inversiones (investments)**
(een-behr-see-on-es)

**WOAH!**

That was a lot to process. I know, I get it, grammar can be difficult to grasp. But don't sweat it, the more you practice the easier it gets. I promise!

If you are having trouble understanding this week's lesson - don't let that stop you from learning other words and phrases in Spanish. You can always come back to this and practice.

MY NOTES

_____

_____

_____

_____

_____

_____

_____

_____

_____

_____

_____

*Write the correct definite article* (***el, la , los , las***)

1. __ dinero
2. __ computadora
3. __ mano
4. __ tiendas
5. __ plato
6. __ persona

7. __ cargador
8. __ dias
9. __ foto
10. __ problema
11. __ arboles
12. __ ciudades

*Match each subject pronoun*

**yo**..........    you (informal)

**tu**    he/him

**usted**    I

**el**    she/her

**ella**    you (formal)

**nosotros** ............    you all

**nosotras** ............ we

**ellos**    they (female)

**ellas**    we (female)

**ustedes**    they

*Write the correct conjugation*

1.
tener – <u>to have</u>

    tengo – _____

    tienes – _____

    tiene – _____

    tenemos – _____

    tienen – _____

2.
saber – <u>to know</u>

    yo sé – _____

    sabes – _____

    sabe – _____

    sabemos – _____

    saben – _____

3.
decir – <u>to say</u>

    digo – _____

    dices – _____

    dice – _____

    decimos – _____

    dicen – _____

4.
ver – <u>to see</u>

    vi – _____

    viste – _____

    vio – _____

    vimos – _____

    vieron – _____

5.
ir – to <u>go</u>

    voy a ir – _____

    vas a ir – _____

    va a ir – _____

    vamos a ir – _____

    van a ir – _____

# Planeador Semanal
## weekly planner

### Semana de:
week of:

**lunes**
Monday

**martes**
tuesday

**miercoles**
Wednesday

**jueves**
thursday

**viernes**
Friday

**sabado**
Saturday

**domingo**
Sunday

Notes
**Notas**

## Cosas que hacer
things to do

## Recordatorio
reminder

TAMALES

# Compliments

Try using these phrases to compliment family, friends, or people you work with.

**La cena estuvo muy rica.**
(lah seh-nah es-too-voh muy ree-kah)
Dinner was really good.

**Todo estuvo padrisimo!**
(toh-doh ehs-too-voh pah-dree-see-moh)
Everything was great/awesome!

**Te luciste!**
(teh loo-sees-teh)
You outdid yourself!

**Tienes buen gusto.**
(tee-en-es bwehn goos-toh)
You have good taste.

**Eres buena gente.**
(ehr-ehs bweh-nah hen-teh)
You're a good person.

**Me gusta como trabajas.**
(meh goos-tah koh-moh trah-bah-hahs)
I like the way you work.

**Nunca me decepcionas.**
(noon-kah meh deh-sep-cion-ahs)
You never disappoint me.

**Eres uno de mis mejores amigos.**
(ehr-ehs oo-noh deh mees meh-ho-rehs ah-mee-gohs)
You're one of my best friends(m)

**Eres una de mis mejores amigas.**
(ehr-ehs oo-nah deh mees meh-ho-rehs ah-mee-gahs)
You're one of my best friends(f)

**Eres uno de mis mejores trabajadores.**
(ehr-ehs oo-noh deh mees meh-ho-rehs trah-bah-hah-doh-rehs)
You are one of my best workers.

**Te valoro a ti y a tu trabajo.**
(teh vah-loh-roh ah tee ee ah too trah-bah-hoh)
I value you and your work.

**Siempre le echas ganas.**
(see-ehm-preh leh eh-chas gah-nahs)
You always try hard.

Try using these phrases to compliment your significant other.

**Eres una belleza.**
(ehr-ehs oo-nah beh-yes-ah)
You're a beauty.

**Te vez presioso / preciosa.**
(teh vehs preh-see-oh-soh)(preh-see-oh-sah)
You look beautiful/precious.

**Te vez muy bien.**
(teh vehs muy byehn)
You look really good.

**Qué bien te queda ese color.**
(keh byehn teh keh-dah es-eh koh-lohr)
That color suits you.

**Se te ve muy bien esa camisa.**
(seh teh veh muy byehn es-ah kah-mee-sah)
That shirt looks really good on you.

**Que bien hueles.**
(keh byehn oo-ehl-ehs)
You smell really good.

**Me gusta estar contigo.**
(meh goos-tah ehs-tahr kohn-tee-goh)
I like being with you.

**Me gusta tu estilo.**
(meh goos-tah too ehs-tee-loh)
I like your style.

**Me gusta tu outfit/vestimenta.**
(meh goos-tah too outifit/vehs-tee-mehn-tah)
I like your outfit.

**Te queda bien.**
(teh keh-dah byehn)
It suits you.

**Siempre luces bien...**
**pero hoy te pasaste.**
(see-ehm-preh loo-sehs byehn...
pehr-oh oy teh pah-sah-steh)
You always look good...
but today you overdid it.

**Normalmente eres guapo / guapa...**
**pero hoy te luciste!**
(nohr-mahl-men-teh ehr-ehs gwah-poh/gwah-pah...
pehr-oh oy teh loo-sees-teh)
You are usually cute/pretty...
but today you outdid yourself.

# Compliments

| eres muy...<br>(ehr-ehs muy) | you are very... |
|---|---|
| **interesante**<br>(een-teh-reh-sahn-teh) | interesting |
| **agradable**<br>(ah-grah-dah-bleh) | nice |
| **simpático/simpática**<br>(seem-pah-tee-koh) (seem-pah-tee-kah) | friendly |
| **profesional**<br>(proh-feh-see-ohnal) | professional |
| **eficiente**<br>(ef-fee-see-en-teh) | efficient |
| **listo/lista**<br>(lees-toh) (lees-tah) | bright/smart |
| **atractivo / atractiva**<br>(ah-trak-tee-boh) (ah-trahk-tee-bah) | attractive |
| **divertido / divertida**<br>(dee-behr-tee-doh) (dee-behr-tee-dah) | fun |
| **guapo / guapa**<br>(gwah-poh) (gwah-pah) | good looking |
| **elegante**<br>(ehl-eh-gahn-teh) | elegant |
| **trabajador/trabajadora**<br>(trah-bah-ha-dohr) (trah-bah-ha-doh-rah) | hard working |
| **lindo / linda**<br>(leen-doh) (leen-dah) | cute, sweet |

| ¿Qué?<br>(keh) | What? |
|---|---|
| ¿Cuándo?<br>(koo-ando) | When? |
| ¿Dónde?<br>(don-deh) | Where? |
| ¿Quién?<br>(kee-en) | Who? |
| ¿Cómo?<br>(ko-moe) | How? |
| ¿Con quién?<br>(kon kee-en) | With who? |

# Conversation starters

Try using these phrases to spark up a conversation

Oye, ¿qué tal? Soy _____ ¿y tú?
(oh-yeh, keh tahl? soy __, ee too?)

Hey, how's it going? I'm_____ , and you?

Buenos días, ¿tienes planes hoy?
(bweh-nohs dee-ahs, tee-ehn-ehs plah-nehs oy)

Good morning, do you have plans today?

¿Sabes dónde está el/la (sustantivo)?
(sah-behs dohn-deh ehs-tah ehl/lah )

Do you know where the (noun) is?

¿Qué te trae por aquí?
(keh teh trah-eh pohr ah-kee)

What brings you here?

¿Conoces a mucha gente aquí?
(koh-noh-sehs ah moo-chah hen-teh ah-kee)

Do you know a lot of people here?

¿Cuánto tiempo llevas aquí?
(kwahn-toh tee-ehm-poh yeh-vahs ah-kee)

How long have you been here?

¿Vienes seguido por aquí?
(byeh-nehs seh-gwee-doh pohr ah-kee)

Do you come here often?

¿Qué piensas de esto / eso?
(keh pee-ehn-sahs deh ehs-toh / eh-so)

What you think about this / that?

¿Qué hora es/son?
(keh or-ah ehs / son)

What time is it?

¿Qué se te antoja?
(keh seh teh ahn-toh-hah)

What are you craving?

Me encantan tus lentes ¿De dónde son?
(meh ehn-kahn-tahn toos lehn-tehs deh dohn-deh sohn)

I love your glasses, where'd you get them?

¿Me puedes hacer un favor?
(meh pweh-dehs ah-sehr oon fah-bohr)

Can you do me a favor?

¿Cuál es tu signo (zodiacal)?
(kwahl ehs too see-gno (soh-dee-ah-kahl)

What's your sign (zodiac)?

¿Te la estás pasando bien?
(teh lah ehs-tahs pah-sahn-doh byehn)

Are you having a good time?

¿Cuál es tu Instagram?
(kwahl ehs too instagram)

What's your Instagram?

¿Me pasas tu número?
(meh pah-sahs too noo-meh-roh)

Can I have your number?

¿Está desocupada esta silla?
(es-tah deh-so-koo-pah-dah es-tah see-yah)

Is this seat empty?

¿Está ocupada esta silla?
(es-tah oh-koo-pah-da es-tah see-yah?)

Is this seat taken?

**Gracias.**
(grah-see-ahs)

Thank you.

**Muchas gracias.**
(moo-chahs grah-see-ahs)

Thank you very much.

**Muchisimas gracias.**
(moo-chee-see-mahs grah-see-ahs)

Thanks a lot.

**Mil gracias.**
(meel grah-see-ahs)

A thousand thanks.

**Gracias de todos modos.**
(grah-see-ahs deh toh-dohs moh-dohs)

Thanks anyway.

**Te lo agradesco de corazon.**
(teh loh ah-grah-desk-oh deh koh-rah-sohn)

Thank you from the bottom of my heart.

**Todo estuvo perfecto,**
  **muchas gracias.**

(toh-doh ehs-too-voh pehr-fek-toh,
 moo-chahs grah-see-ahs)

Everything was perfect,
  thank you so much.

**De nada.**
(deh nah-dah)

You're welcome.

**No es nada.**
(no es nah-dah)

It's was nothing - no trouble.

**No hay de que.**
(no ay deh keh)

It was no bother.

**Con gusto.**
(kon goos- toh)

Happy to help.

**Fue un placer.**
(fweh oon plah-sehr)

My pleasure.

**Adios.**
(ah-dyohs)

Goodbye.

**Te veo.**
(teh veh-oh)

I'll see you.

**Orale pues ahi nos vemos.**
(oh-rah-leh poo-es ah-ee nohs veh-mohs)

Alright, I'll see you then.

**Cuidate.**
(kwee-dah-teh)

Take care.

**Hasta luego.**
(ah-stah lweh-goh)

See you later.

**Nos vemos al rato.**
(nohs veh-mohs ahl rrah-toh)

I'll see you in a bit.

Answer each question

## A que te dedicas?
### What do you do for a living?

Yo soy...
I am...

**or**

Yo trabajo en...
I work in / at....

## Cual es la cosa mas ridícula que as comprado en Amazon?
### What's the craziest thing you've bought on Amazon?

La cosa mas ridicula que e comprado en Amazon es..
The craziest thing I've bought on Amazon is...

**or**

Yo compre...
I bought...

## De donde eres?
### Where are you from?

Soy de...
I am from...

**or**

Vivo en...
I live in...

**or**

Naci en...
I was born in...

## Qué haces cuando no estás trabajando?

### What do you do when you're not working?

Cuando no estoy trabajando yo..

When I'm not working I...

**or**

Cuando yo no estoy en el trabajo me gusta...

When I'm not at work I like...

## Cuales son tus planes para el futuro?

### What are your plans for the future?

Mi plan para el futuro es...

My plan for the future is...

**or**

Mis planes para el futuro son...

My plans for the future are...

## Por qué quieres aprender español?

### Why do you want to learn Spanish?

Quiero aprender español porque....

I want to learn Spanish because...

## Good conversations involve the exchange of energy and emotions.

Try using these responses to match the other persons vibe.

| | |
|---|---|
| **¡Que padre!** (keh pah-threh) | How cool, very cool. |
| **¡Que chido!** (keh chee-doh) | Very awesome, very cool. |
| **Chido.** (chee-doh) | Cool. |
| **Yo también.** (yoh tahm-byehn) | Me too. |
| **¿A poco?** (ah poh-koh) | Really? |
| **¿De veras?** (deh veh-rahs) | Really? |
| **¿Y luego que paso?** (ee lweh-goh keh pah-soh) | Then what happened? |
| **¡No manches!** (noh mahn-ches) | For real?, no way, WTH |
| **¡No mames!** (noh mah-mehs) | For real?, no way, WTH (vulgar) |
| **Wow, suena divertido.** (wow, soo-eh-nah dee-ver-tido) | Wow, sounds fun. |
| **¿Neta?** (neh-tah) | For real? |
| **Tu tienes la razón.** (too tee-ehn-ehs lah rrah-sohn) | You're right. |
| **Estoy deacuerdo contigo.** (ehs-toy deh ah-kweh-r-doh kohn-tee-goh) | I agree with you. |
| **¿Por que dices eso?** (pohr keh dee-sehs es-so) | Why do you say that? |
| **¿Por que dijiste eso?** (pohr keh dee-hees-teh es-soh) | Why did you say that? |
| **Eso es todo.** (es-soh ehs toh-doh) | That is it, that is all. |
| **¡A mi también me paso lo mismo!** (ah mee tahm-byehn meh pah-soh loh mees-moh) | The same thing happened to me! |
| **¿Me estás hablando en serio?** (meh ehs-tahs ah-blahn-doh ehn seh-ree-oh) | Are you (speaking) serious? |

| | |
|---|---|
| **Dejame hablar primero.** (deh-hah-meh ah-blahr pre-meh-roh) | Let me talk first. |
| **Estas haciendo mucho ruido.** (es-tahs ah-see-ehn-doh moo-choh roo-ee-doh) | You're making a lot of noise. |
| **Estas hablando muy fuerte.** (es-tahs ah-blahn-doh muy foo-ehr-teh) | You're talking too loud. |
| **Esto no me agrada.** (es-toh noh meh ah-grah-dah) | I don't like this. |
| **No me hables con ese tono.** (noh meh ah-blehs kohn ehs-eh toh-no) | Don't talk to me in that tone. |
| **Callate.** ( kah-yah-teh) | Shut up. |

# Making Plans

**Te recojo a las 3pm, ¿qué te parece?**
(teh reh-koh-ho ah las trehs , keh teh pah-reh-seh)
**I'll pick you up at 3pm, what do you say?**

**Te invito a comer**
(teh een-vee-toh ah koh-mehr)
**I'll take you out to eat**

**¿Vienes conmigo?**
(byehn-ehs kohn-mee-goh)
**Come with me?**

**¿Qué vas a hacer mañana?**
(keh vahs ah ah-sehr mah-nyah-nah)
**What are you doing tomorrow?**

**Vamos a cenar**
(bah-mohs ah seh-nahr)
**Let's have dinner**

**¿Tienes planes este fin de semana?**
(tee-ehn-ehs plah-nehs ehs-teh feen deh seh-mah-nah)
**Do you have plans this weekend?**

**¿Qué te parecen unos tacos?
Yo invito**
(keh teh pah-reh-sehn oo-nohs tah-kohs
yoh een-vee-toh)
**What do you say we get
tacos? My treat**

**Te gustaria ir...**
(teh goos-tah-ree-ah eer)
**Would you like to go...**

| | |
|---|---|
| **al cine** | to the movies |
| (ahl see-neh) | |
| **al bar** | to the bar |
| (ahl bar) | |
| **al parque** | to the park |
| (ahl pahr-keh) | |
| **al baile** | to the dance |
| (ahl bah-ee-leh) | |
| **de compras** | shopping |
| (deh kohm-prahs) | |
| **a la playa** | to the beach |
| (ah lah plah-yah) | |
| **a comer** | eat |
| (ah koh-mehr) | |
| **a caminar** | on a walk |
| (ah kah-mee-nahr) | |
| **a desayunar** | get breakfast |
| (ah deh-sah-yu-nahr) | |
| **al boliche** | bowling |
| (ahl bohl-ee-cheh) | |
| **a la fiesta** | to the party |
| (ah lah fee-ehs-tah) | |
| **al concierto** | to the concert |
| (ahl kohn-see-ehr-toh) | |

**Creo que sería divertido si fuéramos
juntos a...**
(kreh-oh keh seh-ree-ah dee-behr-tee-doh see
foo-ehr-ah-mohs hoon-tos ah)
**I think it would be fun if we went
together to ...**

**¿Te gustaría ir conmigo?**
(teh goos-tah-ree-ah eer kohn-mee-goh)
**Would you like to go with me?**

**¿Qué te gustaría hacer?**
(keh teh goos-tah-ree-ah ah-sehr)
**What would you like to do?**

## Agreeing to plans

**¡Sí!**
(see)

Yes!

**¡Órale!**
(oh-rah-leh)

Alright!, ok!

**¡Vá!**
(vah)

Ok!, deal!

**Dalo por hecho.**
(dah-loh por eh-choh)

Done deal

**Sí, me parece bien.**
(see, meh pah-reh-seh bee-ehn)

Yes, I like that

**Sí, me encantaría.**
(see, meh ehn-kahn-tah-ree-ah)

Yes, I'd love that

**¡Ya está hecho!**
(yah ehs-tah eh-choh)

It's done!, it's planned!

**¡Me late!**
(meh lah-teh)

I'm feeling it!

**¿A qué hora comienza?**
(ah keh oh-rah koh-mee-ehn-sah)

What time does it start?

¡Ah huevo! means Hell yeah!
Ah Huevo is vulgar.
Depending on the tone and the
expression, it can be a good "hell yeah!"
or it can be a
bad "hell yeah!"

**¿A qué hora? A mí me da igual porque tengo el día libre**
(ah keh oh-rah? Ah mee meh dah ee-gwahl pohr-keh tehn-goh ehl dee-ah lee-breh

**What time? It doesn't matter to me  because I'm free all day**

## Saying NO to plans

**No puedo.**
(noh poo-eh-doh)

I can't

**No, lo siento.**
(noh, loh see-ehn-toh)

No, sorry.

**No voy a poder ir.**
(noh voy ah poh-dehr eer)

I won't be able to make it.

**La verdad es que no me late.**
(lah vehr-dahd ehs keh noh meh lah-teh)

Honestly, I'm not feeling it.

**Gracias, pero no.**
(grah-see-ahs, peh-roh noh)

Thanks, but no.

**Tengo otras cosas que hacer.**
(tehn-goh oh-trahs koh-sahs keh ahs-ehr)

I have other things to do.

**Me encantaría, pero no puedo.**
(meh ehn-kahn-tah-ree-ah, peh-roh no poo-eh-doh)

I would love to but I can't.

**Suena bien, pero no.**
(soo-eh-nah biehn, peh-roh no)

Sounds good, but no.

**Quizás la próxima vez.**
(kee-sahs lah prohk-si-mah vehs)

Maybe next time.

**No tengo ganas.**
(noh tehn-goh gah-nahs)

I don't want to, I don't feel like it

**Ya tengo planes con...**
(yah tehn-goh plah-nehs kohn)

I already have plans with...

**Estoy muy ocupado/ocupada, tal vez otro día.**
(ehs-toy muy oh-koo-pah-doh/oh-koo-pah-dah, tahl vehs oh-troh dee-ah)

I'm really busy, maybe another day.

## Canceling Plans

Se me olvidaron los planes que teníamos, lo siento.
I forgot about our plans, I'm sorry.
(seh meh ol-vee-dah-rohn los plan-es keh teh-nee-ah-mohs, loh see-ehn-toh)

Tengo que cancelar, lo siento.
I have to cancel, I'm sorry.
(tehn-goh keh kahn-seh-lahr, loh see-ehn-toh)

Podemos cambiar los planes para otro día?
Can we change our plans to another day?
(poh-deh-mohs kahm-bahr lohs plah-nehs pah-rah oh-troh dee-ah)

No me siento bien, me voy a quedar a descansar.
I don't feel well, I'm going to stay and rest.
(noh meh see-ehn-toh biehn, meh voy ah keh-dahr ah dehs-kahn-sahr)

Sabes, mejor me voy a quedar en mi casa.
You know, I'm going to stay home instead.
(sah-behs, meh-hor meh voy ah keh-dahr ehn mee kah-sah)

Mi carro se descompuso, no voy a poder ir.
My car broke down, I won't be able to make it.
(mee kar-ro seh dehs-kohm-poo-soh, noh voy ah poh-dehr eer)

## Saying yes

| | | | |
|---|---|---|---|
| **Sí** (see) | Yes | **Ajá** (ah-hah) | Sure, yes |
| **Ok** (okay) | Ok | **No te puedo decir que no** (no teh pweh-doh deh-seer keh no) | I can't say no to you |
| **Sale** (sah-leh) | Alright, ok | **De acuerdo** (deh ah-kwehr-doh) | Agreed |
| **Sip** (seep) | Yup | **Efectivamente** (effek-tee-va-men-teh) | Effectively |
| **Obviamente (obvio)** (oh-vee-ah-men-teh)(oh-vee-oh) | Obviously | **Absolutamente** (ab-so-loo-tah-men-teh) | Absolutely |
| **Por supuesto** (pohr soo-poo-es-toh) | Of course | **Sin duda** (seen doo-dah) | No doubt |
| **¡Claro que sí!** (klah-roh keh see) | Of course! | **Así es** (ah-see es) | That's right |
| **Clarines** (klah-ree-nes) | Sure thing | **¡Eso es!** (eh-soh es) | That's it! |
| **Simon** (see-mon) | Sure | | |

## Saying no

| | | | |
|---|---|---|---|
| **No, gracias** (no grah-see-as) | No, thank you | **Chale** (cha-leh) | Nah |
| **Nop** (nope) | Nope | **No mames!** (no mah-mes) | No way (vulgar) |
| **Nel** (nehl) | No, nah | **No manches!** (no man-ches) | No way |
| **Por supuesto que no** (por sue-poo-es-toh ke- no) | Of course not | | |
| **Claro que no** (cla-ro ke no) | Of course not | | |
| **Para nada** (pa-rah nah-dah) | No way | | |
| **Obviamente no (obvio que no)** (ovbi-ah-men-teh no) | Obviously not | | |

87

# Test your understanding

pregunta
question

respuesta
answer

1. List 3 different ways to say "goodbye" in Spanish.

........................................................

........................................................

........................................................

2. List 3 ways to make plans in Spanish.

........................................................

........................................................

........................................................

3. List 3 ways to say "yes" in Spanish.

........................................................

........................................................

........................................................

4. List 3 ways to say "no" in Spanish.

........................................................

........................................................

........................................................

# MY NOTES

# Planeador Semanal
## Weekly planner

### Semana de:
week of:

| |
|---|

**lunes**
Monday

**martes**
tuesday

**miercoles**
Wednesday

**jueves**
thursday

**viernes**
Friday

**sabado**
Saturday

**domingo**
Sunday

Notes
**Notas**

90

## Cosas que hacer
things to do

## Recordatorio
reminder

## Where is the...?

**¿Dónde está el baño?**
(don-deh ehs-tah ehl bah-nyoh)

**Where is the bathroom?**

**¿Dónde está la entrada?**
(don-deh ehs-tah  lah ehn-trah-dah)

**Where is the entrance?**

**¿Dónde está la salida?**
(don-deh ehs-tah  lah sah-lee-dah)

**Where is the exit?**

**¿Dónde está la tienda?**
(don-deh ehs-tah  lah tee-ehn-dah)

**Where is the store?**

**¿Dónde está la escuela?**
(don-deh ehs-tah lah ehs-kweh-lah)

**Where is the school?**

**¿Dónde está la biblioteca?**
(don-deh ehs-tah  lah bee-blee-yoh-teh-kah)

**Where is the library?**

**¿Dónde está la parada de autobús?**
(don-deh ehs-tah lah pah-rah-dah deh ow-toh-boohs)

**Where is the bus stop?**

**¿Dónde está la estación de tren?**
(don-deh ehs-tah  lah ehs-tah-see-ohn deh trehn)

**Where is the train station?**

**¿Dónde está el mercado?**
(don-deh ehs-tah ehl mehr-ka-doh)

**Where is the grocery store?**

**¿Dónde esta la carniceria?**
(don-deh ehs-tah  lah kahr-nee-seh-ree-ah)

**Where is the butchery?**

**¿Dónde está la panadería?**
(don-deh ehs-tah   lah pah-nah-deh-ree-ah)

**Where is the bakery?**

**¿Dónde está la casa de cambio?**
(don-deh ehs-tah  lah kah-sah deh kahm-bee-oh)

**Where is the currency exchange?**

**¿Dónde está la estación de bomberos?**
(don-deh ehs-tah lah ehs-tah-see-ohn deh bohm-beh-rohs)

**Where is the fire station?**

**¿Dónde está el banco?**
(don-deh ehs-tah  ehl bahn-koh)

**Where is the bank?**

**¿Dónde está el parque?**
(don-deh ehs-tah ehl pahr-keh)

**Where is the park?**

**¿Dónde está el restaurante?**
(don-deh ehs-tah  ehl rehs-tah-oo-rahn-teh)

**Where is the restaurant?**

**¿Dónde está el aeropuerto?**
(don-deh ehs-tah  ehl ah-eh-roh-pwehr-toh)

**Where is the airport?**

## Emergencies

**Necesito ayuda.**
(neh-seh-see-toh ai-you-dah)

I need help

**¡Detente!**
(deh-ten-teh)

Stop!

**¡Fuego!**
(fway-goh)

Fire!

**¡Cuidado!**
(koo-ee-dah-doh)

Watch out!

**Llama a la policía.**
(yah-mah ah lah poh-lee-see-ah)

Call the police.

**Llama a la ambulancia.**
(yah-mah ah lah ahm-boo-lahn-see-ah)

Call the ambulance.

**Es una emergencia.**
(ehs oon-ah eh-mehr-hen-see-ah)

It's an emergency.

**Ha habido un accidente.**
(ah ah-be-doh oon ahk-see-dehn-teh)

There's been an accident.

**¿Dónde está el hospital?**
(dohn-deh ehs-tah ehl oh-spee-tahl)

Where's the hospital?

**¿Dónde está la clínica?**
(dohn-deh ehs-tah lah klee-nee-kah)

Where is the clinic?

**¿Dónde está la farmacia?**
(dohn-deh ehs-tah lah fahr-mah-see-ah)

Where's the pharmacy?

**¿Dónde está la estación de policía?**
(dohn-deh ehs-tah lah esta-cion deh poli-cia)

Where is the police station?

**Quiero reportar un delito.**
(kee-eh-roh reh-pohr-tahr oon deh-lee-toh)

I want to report an offence.

**He perdido mi...**
(eh pehr-dee-doh mee)

I lost my...

## Tourism

**¿Cuál es la mejor manera de moverse por la ciudad ?**
(kwahl ehs lah meh-hohr mahn-eh-rah deh moh-behr-seh pohr lah see-dahd)

What is the best way to get around the city?

**¿Hay algún restaurante o café cerca?**
(ahy al-goon rehs-tah-oo-rahn-teh oh kah-feh sehr-kah)

Are there any restaurants or cafes near

**¿Hay alguna playa o parque cerca?**
(ahy al-goo-nah bweh-nah playah oh pahr-keh sehr-kah)

Are there any beaches or parks close by

**¿Hay alguna oferta o descuento?**
(ahy al-goo-nah oh-fehr-tah oh dehs-kwehn-toh)

Are there any good deals or discounts?

**¿Hay algún sitio que deba visitar?**
(ahy al-goon see-tioh keh deh-bah vee-sytahr)

Is there any site that I should visit?

**¿Hay alguna zona de compras o mercados en el área?**

Are there any shopping centers or markets in the area?

(ahy al-goo-nah zoh-nah deh kohm-prahs oh mehr-kah-dohs ehn ehl ah-reh-ah)

**¿Hay buenos lugares para alojarse en el área ?**

Are there any good places to stay in the area?

(ahy bweh-nohs loo-gah-rehs pah-rah ah-loh-hahr-seh ehn ehl ah-reh-ah)

**¿Hay buenos lugares para comer?**

Are there any good places to eat?

(ahy bweh-nohs loo-gah-rehs pah-rah koh-mehr)

**¿Hay buenos lugares para salir por la noche?**

Are there any good places to go out at night?

(ahy bweh-nohs loo-gah-rehs pah-rah sah-leer pohr lah noh-cheh)

**¿Hay opciones para actividades al aire libre/afuera?**

Are there any options for outdoor activities?

(ahy ohp-see-oh-nehs pah-rah akt-ee-vee-dahd-ehs ahl ah-ee-reh lee-breh)

**¿Hay alguna visita guiada o actividad en la que pueda participar?**

(ahy al-goo-nah vee-sytah gee-ah-dah oh akt-ee-vee-dahd ehn lah keh pweh-dah par-tee-see-pahr)

**Are there any guided tours or activities that I can participate in?**

**¿Hay algún festival o evento mientras estoy en la ciudad?**

(ahy ahl-goon fes-teeh-vahl oh eh-vehn-toh meen-trah ehs-toy ehn lah see-oo-dad)

**Are there any festivals or events happening while I'm in town?**

**museos - museums**
(moo-seh-ohs)
**galerias - galleries**
(gah-leh-ree-ahs)
**bolos - bowling**
(boh-lohs)
**bar - bar**
(bar)
**discoteca - nightclub**
(dees-koh-teh-kah)
**lugares de música en vivo - live music venues**
(loo-gah-rehs deh moo-see-kah ehn vee-boh)

♦

**caminando - walking**
(kah-mee-nahn-doh)
**corriendo - running**
(koh-ree-ehn-doh)
**bicicleta - bicycle**
(beeh-see-kleh-tah)
**autobus - bus**
(ow-toh-boos)
**taxi- taxi**
(taxi)
**carro rentado - rental car**
(kar-roh ren-ta-doh)

**derecho -straight**
(deh-reh-choh)
**atras - back**
(ah-trahs)
**derecha - right**
(deh-reh-chah)
**izquierda - left**
(ees-keer-dah)
**a lado - on the side**
(ah lah-doh)

## Airport

**Tengo un vuelo a (ciudad/país) a las (hora).**   I have a flight to (city/country) at (time).
(tehn-goh oon vweh-loh ah (see-oo-dahd/pah-yees) ah lahs (oh-rah))

**¿Puedo hacer el check-in, por favor?**   Can I check in, please?
(pweh-doh ah-sehr ehl check-in, pohr fah-vohr)

**¿Puedo tener un boleto de abordaje?**   Can I have a boarding pass, please?
(pweh-doh teh-nehr oon bol-eh-toh deh ah-bohr-dah-heh)

**¿Dónde está mi equipaje?**   Where is my luggage?
(dohn-deh ehs-tah mee eh-kee-pah-heh)

**¿Puedo cambiar mi vuelo, por favor?**   Can I change my flight, please?
(pweh-doh kahm-be-ahr mee vweh-loh pohr fah-vohr)

**¿Puedo actualizar a primera clase?**   Can I upgrade to first class?
(pweh-doh ahk-twah-lee-zahr ah pree-meh-rah klah-seh)

**¿Me puede traer un carrito, por favor?**   Can I have a luggage cart/trolley, please?
(meh pweh-deh trah-ehr oon kah-ree-toh, pohr fah-vohr)

**Necesito una silla de ruedas, por favor.**   I need a wheelchair, please.
(neh-seh-see-toh oo-nah see-yah deh rweh-dahs, pohr fah-vohr)

**Estoy esperando mi taxi/Uber.**   I am waiting on my taxi/uber.
(eh-stoy ehs-peh-rahn-doh mee taxi/uber)

**Necesito un taxi.**   I need a taxi.
(neh-seh-see-toh oon taxi)

# Planeador Semanal
### Weekly planner

## Semana de:
### Week of:

**lunes**
Monday

**martes**
Tuesday

**miercoles**
Wednesday

**jueves**
Thursday

**viernes**
Friday

**sabado**
Saturday

**domingo**
Sunday

Notes
**Notas**

## Cosas que hacer
### Things to do

## Recordatorio
### reminder

95

¿Me puede traer una silla alta para un niño?　　Can you bring a high-chair for a child?
(meh pweh-deh trah-ehr oo-nah see-yah ahl-tah pa-rah oon nee-nyo)

¿Puedo pedir una sala / mesa privada,　　Can I ask for have a private room/table please?
　por favor?
(pweh-doh peh-deer oo-nah sah-lah / meh-sah pree-ba-dah,
pohr fah-vohr)

¿Tiene disponible una mesa con vista?　　Do you have a table with a view available?
(tee-eh-neh dis-poni-ble oo-nah meh-sah kohn vees-tah)

　　al aire libre - outdoors
　　(al ah-ee-re lee-breh)
　　cerca a la chimenea - near the fireplace
　　(ser-ka ah la chee-meh-neah)

¿Nos puede dar un menú vegano, por favor?　　Can we have a vegan menu, please?
(nohs pweh-deh dahr oon meh-noo vay-gahn-oh, pohr fah-vohr)

　　vegetariano - vegetarian
　　(beh-heh-ta-ree-ah-no)
　　sin gluten - gluten-free
　　(sin gloo-ten)

La comida está caliente.　　The food is hot.
(lah co-mee-dah ehs-tah kah-lee-en-teh)
El pollo está frío.　　The chicken is cold.
(ehl poh-yoh ehs-tah free-oh)
La carne está cruda.　　The meat is raw.
(lah kahr-neh ehs-tah kroo-dah)
Está picante.　　It's spicy.
(ehs-tah pee-kahn-teh)
Sabe dulce.　　Tastes sweet.
(sah-beh dool-seh)
Está un poco salado.　　It's a little salty.
(ehs-tah oon poh-koh sah-lah-doh)

## Condiments

| | |
|---|---|
| **sal** (sal) | salt |
| **pimienta** (pee-me-en-tah) | pepper |
| **azucar** (ah-zoo-car) | sugar |
| **salsa picante** (salsa pee-kahn-teh) | hot sauce |
| **mayonesa** (mah-yo-nesa) | mayonnaise |
| **mostaza** (mos-tah-zah) | mustard |
| **ketchup** (ket-choop) | ketchup |

## Flavors

| | |
|---|---|
| **salado** (sala-doh) | salty |
| **dulce** (dool-seh) | sweet |
| **picante** (pee-kahn-teh) | spicy |
| **acido** (ah-see-doh) | sour |
| **amargo** (ah-mar-go) | bitter |

## Drinks

| | |
|---|---|
| **agua** (ah-gwah) | water |
| **jugo** (hoo-go) | juice |
| **licuado** (lee-koo-ah-doh) | smoothie |
| **malteada** (mal-teh-ada) | milkshake |
| **aguas frescas** (ah-gwahs fres-kahs) | fresh fruit juice |
| **agua de horchata** (ah-gwah deh or-cha-tah) | sweet rice water |
| **refresco (sin hielo)** (reh-fresco (sin ee-ello) | soda (with no ice) |
| **leche** (leh-che) | milk |
| **coca** (ko-ka) | coca cola |
| **limonada** (lee-mona-dah) | lemonade |
| **chocolate caliente** (choco-lah-teh kah-lee-en-teh) | hot chocolate |

## Dessert

| | |
|---|---|
| **pastel** (pah-s-tel) | cake |
| **pastelito** (pah-s-tel-ito) | cupcake |
| **galleta** (gha-ye-tah) | cookie |
| **gelatina** (hella-tina) | jello |
| **helado** (eh-lah-doh) | ice cream |

## Dine in

**Hola, tenemos una reservacion para dos a las 7.**

(oh-la, teh-ne-mos una reh-ser-va-cion pah-ra dos ah las sie-teh (deh la tar-deh)

Hi, we have a reservation for two at 7.

**¿Puedo ver el menú, por favor?**

(pweh-do ver ehl me-nu, por fa-vor)

Can I see a menu, please?

**¿Me puede dar un vaso de agua, por favor?**

(me pweh-de dar un va-so deh a-gwa, por fa-vor)

Can I have a glass of water, please?

**¿Puede volver a llenar nuestras bebidas, por favor?**

(pweh-de vol-ver ah ye-nar nues-tras beh-bee-das, por fa-vor)

Can you refill our drinks, please?

**¿Alguna recomendación?**

(al-goo-na reh-co-men-da-cion)

Any recommendations?

**¿Me puede dar el plato de mole, por favor?**

(me pweh-de dar ehl pla-toh deh mo-leh, por fa-vor)

Can I get the plate of mole, please?

**¿Me puede traer una caja para llevar, por favor?**

(meh pweh-deh trah-er una ca-ha pah-ra ye-var, por fa-vor)

Can I have a to-go box, please?

**¿Puede traerme la cuenta, por favor?**
(pweh-de tra-ehr-meh lah coo-en-tah, por fa-vor)

Can you bring me the check/bill, please?

**¿Me puede dar más de esto?**

(me pweh-deh dar mas deh es-toh)

Can you give me more of this?

**¿Me puede traer otro de esto?**

(meh pweh-deh trah-ehr oh-tro deh es-toh)

Can you bring me another of these?

**¿Puede traernos algunos utensilios?**

(pwe-de trah-er-nos al-goo-nos u-ten-si-lee-os)

Can you bring us some utensils?

> **cuchara - spoon**
> (koo-cha-rah)
>
> **tenedor - fork**
> (teh-nedor)
>
> **cuchillo - knife**
> (koo-chee-yo)
>
> **servilletas - napkins**
> (ser-vee-ye-tas)

## Coffee shop

**¿Puedo ver el menú, por favor? - Can I see the menu, please?**
(pwe-doh ver el meh-nóo, por fa-vor)

**¿Me puede dar un café? - Can I have a coffee?**
(pwe-doh ten-er un ka-feh)

**té - tea**
(teh)
**latte - latte**
(lah-teh)
**cappuccino -cappuccino**
(kappu-chee-no)
**espresso - espresso**
(espresso)

**Me puede dar un pequeño - Can I have a small**

(meh pue-des dar un peh-ke-nyo)

**mediano - medium**
(medi-ah-no)
**grande - large**
(gran-deh)
**extra grande - extra large**
(extra gran-deh)

**sin cafeína - decaf**
(seen kah-fey-eena)
**sin lacteos - non dairy**
(seen lak-teh-os)
**leche de soya - soy milk**
(leh-che deh soy-ah)
**leche de almendra - almond milk**
(leh-che deh al-men-drah
**crema para café - coffee creamer**
(kre-mah pah-rah ka-feh)
**endulzante - sweetner**
(en-dool-zan-teh)

## Bar

**cerveza - beer**
(ser-veh-sa)
**chela - beer**
(che-lah)
**caguama - a 32 oz or 40oz beer bottle**
(ka-goo-ah-mah)
**vino - wine**
(vee-no)
**coctel - cocktail**
(cok-tel)
**un trago - a shot**
(un tra-go)
**botella - bottle**
(boh-teh-yah)
**limon y sal - lime and salt**
(lee-mon ee sal)
**tequila - tequila**
(teh-kee-lah)

## Fast food

**Me puede dar un numero dos con sprite, por favor?**   Can I get a number two with sprite, please?
(meh pue-deh dar oon noo-mero dos kon sprite por fa-vor)
**Para llevar**                                          To go, takeout
(pah-ra ye-var)

**una hamburguesa - a hamburger**
(oon-ah ambur-gues-ah)
**un perro caliente - a hot dog**
(oon peh-rro ka-lien-teh
**unas papas - potatoes / fries**
(oon-ahs pah-pahs)

**pollo frito - fried chicken**
(poh-yo free-toh)
**alitas de pollo - chicken wings**
 (ali-tas deh poh-yo)

## verduras
### vegetables

| | |
|---|---|
| **Zanahorias** (sah-nah-oh-ree-ahs) | Carrots |
| **Cebollas** (seh-boh-yahs) | Onions |
| **Tomates** (toh-mah-tehs) | Tomatoes |
| **Papas** (pah-pahs) | Potatoes |
| **Pimientos** (pee-mee-ehn-tohs) | Bell peppers |
| **Pepinos** (peh-pee-nohs) | Cucumbers |
| **Lechuga** (leh-choo-gah) | Lettuce |
| **Brócoli** (broh-koh-lee) | Broccoli |
| **Maíz** (mah-eez) | Corn |
| **Habichuelas** (ah-bee-choo-eh-lahs) | Peas |
| **Espárragos** (eh-spah-rrah-gohs) | Asparagus |
| **Berenjena** (beh-rehn-heh-nah) | Eggplant |
| **Calabacín** (kah-lah-bah-seen) | Zucchini |
| **Coliflor** (koh-lee-flohr) | Cauliflower |
| **Betabeles** (beh-tah-beh-lehs) | Beets |
| **Rábanos** (rah-bahn-ohs) | Radishes |
| **Alcachofas** (ahl-kah-choh-fahs) | Artichokes |
| **Hongos** (ohn-gohs) | Mushrooms |
| **Kale** (kah-leh) | Kale |
| **Espinacas** (eh-spee-nah-kahs) | Spinach |
| **Repollo** (reh-poh-yoh) | Cabbage |
| **Coles de Bruselas** (koh-lehs deh broo-seh-lahs) | Brussels sprouts |

## frutas
### fruits

| | |
|---|---|
| **Manzanas** (mahn-sah-nahs) | Apples |
| **Plátanos** (plah-tah-nohs) | Bananas |
| **Naranjas** (nah-rahn-hah-s) | Oranges |
| **Fresas** (freh-sahs) | Strawberries |
| **Uvas** (ooh-vahs) | Grapes |
| **Melones** (meh-loh-nehs) | Melons |
| **Piña** (pee-nyah) | Pineapple |
| **Mango** (mahn-goh) | Mango |
| **Duraznos** (doo-rahs-nohs) | Peaches |
| **Ciruelas** (cee-rue-eh-lahs) | Plums |
| **Cerezas** (seh-reh-zas) | Cherries |
| **Kiwi** (kiwi) | Kiwi |
| **Arándanos** (ah-rahn-dah-nohs) | Blueberries |
| **Frambuesas** (frahm-boo-eh-sahs) | Raspberries |
| **Moras** (moh-rahs) | Blackberries |
| **Papaya** (pah-pah-yah) | Papaya |
| **Sandía** (sahn-dee-ah) | Watermelon |
| **Melón** (meh-lohn) | Cantaloupe |
| **Melón miel** (meh-lohn myel) | Honeydew |
| **Peras** (peh-rahs) | Pears |
| **Albaricoques** (ahl-bah-ree-koh-kehs) | Apricots |
| **Granadas** (grah-nah-dahs) | Pomegranates |
| **Mandarinas** (mahn-dah-ree-nahs) | Mandarins |
| **Limón** (lee-mohn) | Lemon |
| **Toronja** (toh-rohn-hah) | Grapefruit |

## In the kitchen

| | |
|---|---|
| **refrigerador** (reh-free-hera-dohr) | refrigerator |
| **congelador** (kohn-heh-la-dohr) | frezeer |
| **estufa** (eh-stoo-fah) | stove |
| **fregadero** (fre-gah-deh-roh) | sink |
| **microondas** (mee-kro-on-dahs) | microwave |
| **tostador** (tos-tah-dohr) | toaster |
| **despensa** (des-pen-sah) | pantry |
| **licuadora** (lee-kwa-doh-rah) | blender |
| **sartén** (sar-ten) | frying pan |
| **olla** (oyah) | pot |
| **pinzas** (peen-sahs) | tongs |
| **tabla de cortar** (tah-blah de kor-tar) | cutting board |
| **espátula** (es-pa-too-lah) | spatula |
| **platillo** (pla-tee-yoh) | plate |
| **tazón** (tah-sohn) | bowl |
| **vaso** (vah-soh) | glass |
| **taza** (tah-sah) | cup |
| **trastes** (tras-tehs) | dishes |
| **jabón de trastes** (hah-bohn deh tras-tehs) | dish soap |

| | |
|---|---|
| **cocina** (koh-seen-ah) | kitchen |
| **cocinar** (koh-seen-ar) | to cook |
| **cocinero/cocinera** (koh-seen-eh-ro)/(koh-seen-eh-rah) | cook (person) |
| **ingredientes** (een-gre-dee-en-tehs) | ingredients |
| **receta** (reh-se-tah) | recipe |
| **mezclar** (mehs-klar) | to mix |
| **picar** (pee-kar) | to chop |
| **rallar** (rah-yar) | to grate |
| **pelar** (peh-lar) | to peel |
| **cocer** (koh-ser) | to boil |
| **hornear** (or-neh-ar) | to bake |
| **freír** (frey-eer) | to fry |
| **asar** (ah-sar) | to roast |
| **a la parrilla** (ah la par-ee-ya) | to grill |
| **aderezo** (ah-deh-reh-so) | dressing |
| **salsa** (salh-sa) | sauce |
| **condimentos** (kon-dee-men-tohs) | condiments |

**Huele muy bien aquí.**

(oo-eh-leh muy byen ah-kee)

Smells really good in here.

**Tengo ganas de sushi/comida mexicana/comida china.**

(ten-go gah-nahs deh sushi / koh-mee-dah meh-he-kah-nah / koh-mee-dah chee-nah)

I'm craving sushi/Mexican/Chinese food.

**Estoy cocinando la cena.**

(es-toy ko-see-nahn-doh lah seh-nah)

I am cooking dinner.

**¿Quieres ayudarme a preparar la cena?**

(kee-eres ah-you-dahr-meh ah pre-pah-rahr lah seh-nah)

Do you want to help me prepare dinner?

**Necesito comprar más ingredientes para la receta.**

(neh-seh-see-toh kohm-prahr mahs een-greh-dyen-tes pah-rah lah reh-seh-tah)

I need to buy more ingredients for the recipe.

**¿Me ayudas a mezclar los ingredientes?**

(meh ah-yoo-dahs a meh-zklar los een-greh-dyen-tes)

Can you help me mix the ingredients?

**Necesito picar las cebollas antes de cocinar.**

(neh-seh-see-toh pee-kahr lahs seh-boh-yahs ahn-tehs deh ko-see-nahr)

I need to chop the onions before cooking.

**Voy a rallar el queso para la pizza.**

(voy a rah-yar el keh-so pah-rah lah pizza)

I am going to grate the cheese for the pizza.

**Pelé las papas antes de freírlas.**

(peh-leh lahs pah-pahs ahn-tehs deh frey-eer-lahs)

I peeled the potatoes before frying them.

**Estoy cocinando la carne en la parrilla.**

(es-toy ko-see-nahn-doh lah kahr-neh en lah par-ee-yah)

I am cooking the meat on the grill.

**Preparé un aderezo de mostaza y miel para la ensalada.**

(pre-pah-reh oon ah-deh-reh-soh deh moh-stah-sah ee myehl pah-rah lah ehn-sah-lah-dah)

I made a mustard and honey dressing for the salad.

**La salsa de tomate está lista.**

(lah sal-sah deh toh-mah-teh es-tah lees-tah)

The tomato sauce is ready.

**No se te olvide ponerle condimentos al pozole.**

(noh seh teh ol-vee-deh poh-nehr-leh kohn-dy-men-tohs ahl pozole)

Don't forget to put seasoning on the hominy soup.

**Yo voy a lavar los trastes.**

(yoh voy a lah-var los trah-stehs)

I'll do the dishes.

**Por favor, lava los trastes.**

(por fah-vor, lah-vah los trah-stehs)

Please, do the dishes.

**¿Debo poner esto en el refrigerador?**

(deh-boh po-ner es-toh ehn el reh-free-hera-dohr)

Should I put this in the refrigerator?

# UNIDADES DE MEDIDA
## units of measurement

**una taza (1 cup)**
(oo-nah tah-sah)

**media taza (1/2 cup)**
(meh-dee-ah tah-sah)

**una cucharada (1 tablespoon)**
(oo-nah koo-chah-rah-dah)

**media cucharada (1/2 tablespoon)**
(meh-dee-ah koo-chah-rah-dah)

**una cucharadita (1 teaspoon)**
(oo-nah koo-chah-rah-dee-tah)

**media cucharadita (1/2 teaspoon)**
(meh-dee-ah koo-chah-rah-dee-tah)

**un litro (1 liter)**
(oon lee-troh)

**medio litro (1/2 liter)**
(meh-dee-oh lee-troh)

**un gramo (1 gram)**
(oon grah-moh)

**medio gramo (1/2 gram)**
(meh-dee-oh grah-moh)

**una onza (1 ounce)**
(oo-nah ohn-sah)

**media onza (1/2 ounce)**
(meh-dee-ah ohn-sah)

**una libra (1 pound)**
(oo-nah lee-brah)

**media libra (1/2 pound)**
(meh-dee-ah lee-brah)

**una pizca (a pinch)**
(oo-nah pees-kah)

**una cuarta parte (1/4)**
(oo-nah kwar-tah pahr-teh)

**una tercera parte (1/3)**
(oo-nah tehr-seh-rah pahr-teh)

**una media (1/2)**
(oo-nah meh-dee-ah)

**metro  - meter**
(meh-troh)

**centímetro - centimeter**
(sehn-tee-meh-troh)

**milímetro - millimeter**
(mee-lee-meh-troh)

**kilómetro - kilometer**
(kee-loh-meh-troh)

**pulgada - inch**
(pool-gah-dah)

**pie - foot**
(pee-eh)

**yarda - yard**
(yahr-dah)

**millas - mile**
(mee-yas)

**kilogramo - kilogram**
(kee-loh-grah-moh)

**Grados Celsius - degrees Celsius**
(grah-dohs sehl-see-ohs)

**Grados Fahrenheit - degrees Fahrenheit**
(grah-dohs fah-rehn-heyt)

# THIS IS HOW I ORDER MY FAVORITE FOOD IN SPANISH

# Planeador Semanal
## weekly planner

**Semana de:**
week of:

| |
|---|

### lunes
Monday

### martes
tuesday

### miercoles
Wednesday

### jueves
Thursday

### viernes
Friday

### sabado
Saturday

### domingo
Sunday

## Cosas que hacer
things to do

## Recordatorio
reminder

Notes
**Notas**

105

Mexico has an estimated population of over 132 million people.

Mexico is known for its warm and friendly people, who often greet each other with a handshake, a hug, or kiss on the cheek.

The Mexican flag consists of three vertical stripes:
green, white, & red. The green stripe represents hope and the independence movement, the white stripe represents purity and unity, and the red stripe represents the blood of the national heroes.

Mexico is famous for its cuisine, which is influenced by a blend of indigenous and European traditions. Some of the most popular dishes in Mexico include tacos, burritos, enchiladas, and mole.

The currency of Mexico is the Mexican peso.

Mexico has a rich artistic and cultural heritage, and is known for its vibrant music, dance, and art scenes. Traditional Mexican music and dance styles include mariachi, ranchera, and jarabe tapatío.

Mexico is also home to many world-class universities and research institutions, and has a growing reputation as a center for higher education and research.

Mexico is a diverse and multicultural country, and as such, many different languages are spoken, but most of the population speaks Spanish. In addition to the Spanish language, indigenous languages are also spoken, including Nahuatl, Yucatec Maya, Mixtec, Zapotec, and Tzotzil, among others.

English, French, German, Chinese, Korean, and Arabic are common languages practiced in Mexico.

The variety of languages spoken in Mexico reflects the country's rich cultural heritage and history.

## Mexico is made up of 31 states

Aguascalientes
Baja California,
Baja California Sur
Campeche
Chiapas
Chihuahua
Coahuila
Colima
Durango
Guanajuato
Guerrero
Hidalgo
Jalisco
México
Michoacán
Morelos
Nayarit
Nuevo León
Oaxaca
Puebla
Querétaro
Quintana Roo
San Luis Potosí
Sinaloa
Sonora
Tabasco
Tamaulipas
Tlaxcala
Veracruz
Yucatán
Zacatecas

## Spanish music genres

Banda
Cumbia
Ranchera
Corridos
Mariachi
Zapateado
Reggaeton
Tribal Guarachero
Duranguense
Norteño
Salsa
Bachata
Pop Latino
Merengue
Rock en Español

## Made in Mexico

Agave, which is used to make tequila, is native to Mexico. The cactus, called "nopal" is also native to Mexico. It is used in traditional dishes and has many medicinal properties.
The Mexican hairless dog, also known as the "Xoloitzcuintli" is an ancient breed that is native to Mexico.

## Mexican food

tacos
burritos
quesadillas
tortas
salsa
guacamole
pico de gallo
carne asada
birria
carnitas
mole
pozole
gorditas
enchiladas
sopes
empanadas
flautas
chilaquiles
huevos rancheros
tostadas
frijoles
nopales
caldo de poyo
menudo
chiles rellenos
ceviche
flan
concha
churros
tamales
atole
chocolate caliente
elotes
mangonada
chicharones

**Feliz cumpleaños!**
(feh-liz koom-pleh-anyos)

**Happy birthday!**

**Te deseo todo lo mejor en tu día especial.**
(teh deh-seh-oh toh-doh lo meh-hor en to dee-ah es-peh-syal)

**I wish you all the best on your special day.**

**Espero que tu cumpleaños sea tan maravilloso como tú.**
(es-peh-roh ke too koom-pleh-a-nyos seh-ah tan mah-rah-vee-yo-so como too)

**I hope your birthday is as wonderful as you are.**

**Que este año te traiga mucha felicidad y éxitos.**
(ke es-teh a-nyo teh tra-ee-gah moo-cha feh-lee-see-dahd ee ex-ee-tohs)

**May this year bring you much happiness and success.**

**Quiero desearte un feliz cumpleaños**
(kee-ero deh-seh-arh-teh oon feh-lis koom-pleh-anyos)

**I want to wish you a happy birthday.**

**Disfruta tu día y que todos tus deseos se hagan realidad**
(dis-fru-tah to dee-ah ee ke toh-dos toos deh-seh-os seh ah-gahn reh-ah-lee-dahd)

**Enjoy your day & may all your wishes come true.**

## Las mañanitas - Birthday song

**Estas son las mañanitas**
**que cantaba el rey David.**
**Hoy por ser día de tu santo**
**te las cantamos aquí.**
**Despierta mi bien despierta**
**Mira que ya amaneció**
**Ya los pajaritos cantan**
**La luna ya se metió.**

These are "Las mañanitas"
that King David sang.
Today being your saint day (or birthday)
we sing [this song] here.
Wake up, my dear, wake up
See, it's morning already
The birds are singing
and the moon has set.

## Quinceañera

A quinceañera is a young woman's 15th birthday celebration. It is a traditional coming-of-age celebration that marks the transition from childhood to womanhood. Quinceañeras are typically celebrated with a formal party which include the birthday girl wearing a traditional quinceañera dress. There's food, dancing, music, and sometimes live bands. The young woman celebrating her quinceañera is typically accompanied by a chambelan (male escort) and damas (female attendants). May also include religious ceremonies or rituals.

"Que le muerda, que le muerda" which translates to "bite it, bite it" is often chanted when the birthday person is ready to bite into their birthday cake.

**Diminutives are very common in Spanish.**
Diminutives are suffixes that indicate small size, youth, and affection.

Some common diminutive suffixes in Spanish include -ito/-ita, -cito/-cita, and -ico/-ica.

| | | |
|---|---|---|
| **tacos** | **taquitos** | little tacos |
| **salsa** | **salsita** | llittle salsa |
| **cafe** | **cafecito** | little coffee |
| **sopa** | **sopita** | little soup |
| **pedazo** | **pedacito** | little piece |
| **pan** | **panesito** | little bread |
| **tortilla** | **tortillita** | little tortilla |
| **manzana** | **manzanita** | little apple |
| **amor** | **amorcito** | little love |
| **besos** | **besitos** | little kisses |
| **muñeca/muñeco** | **muñequita(o)** | little doll |
| **hermano** | **hermanito** | little brother |
| **hermana** | **hermanita** | little sister |
| **amigo/amiga** | **amiguito/amiguita** | little friend |
| **gato** | **gatito** | kitten |
| **regalo** | **regalito** | little present |
| **casa** | **casita** | little house |
| **mesa** | **mesita** | little table |
| **cobija** | **cobijita** | little blanket |
| **botas** | **botitas** | little boots |
| **bolsa** | **bolsita** | little bag |
| **aretes** | **aretitos** | little earrings |

**Oftentimes, if your name is Jesus, you will go by Chuy or Chucho**

| | |
|---|---|
| **Alberto / Roberto** | Beto |
| **Ignacio** | Nacho |
| **Jose** | Pepe, Chepe |
| **Luis / Mauricio** | Whicho |
| **Salvador** | Chava |
| **Vicente** | Chente |
| **Feliciano** | Chano |
| **Guillermo** | Memo |
| **Eduardo / Gerardo** | Lalo |
| **Enrique** | Quique |
| **Antonio** | Toño |
| **Francisco** | Pancho, Kiko, Cisco, Paco |
| **Francisca** | Pancha, Kika, Cisca |
| **Isabella / Isabel** | Chavela |
| **Araceli** | Cheli |
| **Guadalupe** | Lupe, Lupita |
| **Dolores** | Lola |
| **Mercedes** | Meche |
| **Graciela** | Chela |
| **Maria Luisa / Alicia** | Licho |
| **Rosario** | Chayo |
| **Asuncion** | Chona |
| **Antonia** | Toña |

## Jaripeo

A Jaripeo is a traditional Mexican rodeo-style event. The word "jaripeo" comes from the Spanish word "jaripear," which means to ride a horse or a bull.

The event is characterized by its energetic and lively atmosphere, which includes live bands, dancing, food, and entertainment.

## Holidays

**Año nuevo** (New year's day) - January 1
**Dia de los Reyes** (Kings' day) - January 6
**Día del amor y la amistad** (Valentine's day) - February 14
**Semana Santa** (Holy Week) - Easter week
**Pascua** - Easter
**Dia del niño** (children's day) - April 30
**Cinco de Mayo** (Battle of Puebla celebration) - May 5
**Dia de las Madres** (Mother's day) - May 10
**Dia del Padre** (Father's day) - 3rd Sunday of June
**Dia de la Independecia de Mexico** (indepence day) - September 16
**Dia de los muertos** (Day of the dead) - November 2
**Dia de la Virgen de Guadalupe** (Day of the Virgin of Guadalupe) - December 12
**Noche Buena** ( Christmas Eve) - December 24
**Navidad** (Christmas) - December 25
**Vispera de Año Nuevo** (New Year's Eve) - December 31

## Dia de los Muertos

Día de los Muertos, or Day of the Dead, is a Mexican holiday that takes place on November 1st and 2nd. It is a time to celebrate and remember loved ones who have passed away. To remember and honor the dead, rather than mourn them. The celebration typically involves creating alters decorated with candles, marigold flowers, pictures and other symbolic items. People also gather around to share stories, food, and music. The celebration is a way to celebrate the dead and keep their spirits alive in our hearts.

## Week 1

**Write the correct translation**
1. hand
2. face
3. legs
4. mouth
5. muscles
6. head
7. blue
8. purple
9. red
10. green
11. yellow
12. pink

**Match each number**

1 - uno
28 - veintiocho
40 - cuarenta
13 - trece
11- once

**Match each day of the week**

lunes - Monday
martes- Tuesday
miercoles - Wednesday
jueves - Thursday
viernes - Friday
sabado - Saturday
domingo - Sunday

**Write the correct number**
1. *tres*
2. *doce*
3. *trescientos cuarenta y dos*
4. *novecientos seis*
5. *mil veintinueve*
6. *cuatro mil cuatrocientos setenta y uno*
7. *584,200*
8. *267.984*
9. *145*
10. *6,000*

## Week 4

**Write the correct definite article**
1. el
2. la
3. la
4. las
5. el
6. la
7. el
8. los
9. la
10. el
11. los
12. las

**Match each subject pronoun**

yo - I
tu - you(informal)
usted - you (formal)
el - he/him
ella - she /her
nosotros - we
nosotras - we(female)
ellos - they
ellas - they(female)
ustedes(you-all)

**Write the correct conjugation**

1. to have
   I have
   you have
   he/she/it has
   we have
   they have

2. to know
   I know
   you know
   he/she/it knows
   we know
   they know

3. to say
   I say
   you say
   he/she/it says
   we say
   they say

4. to see
   I saw
   you saw
   he/she/it saw
   we saw
   they saw

5. to go
   I will go
   you will go
   he/she/it will go
   we will go
   they will go

# MY NOTES

Made in United States
Orlando, FL
26 May 2025

61420444R00063